BALANCED
LEADERSHIP
––––––––– *for* –––––––––
Powerful Learning

BALANCED
LEADERSHIP
— *for* —
Powerful Learning

TOOLS FOR ACHIEVING SUCCESS
IN YOUR SCHOOL

Bryan Goodwin & Greg Cameron *with* Heather Hein

Alexandria, Virgina USA

Denver, Colorado USA

1703 N. Beauregard St. • Alexandria, VA 22311-1714 USA
Phone: 800-933-2723 or 703-578-9600 • Fax: 703-575-5400
Website: www.ascd.org • E-mail: member@ascd.org
Author guidelines: www.ascd.org/write

Deborah S. Delisle, *Executive Director;* Stefani Roth, *Publisher;* Genny Ostertag, *Director, Content Acquisitions;* Julie Houtz, *Director, Book Editing & Production;* Darcie Russell, *Senior Associate Editor;* Thomas Lytle, *Senior Graphic Designer;* Mike Kalyan, *Manager, Production Services;* Keith Demmons, *Production Designer;* Kelly Marshall, *Senior Production Specialist*

McREL INTERNATIONAL

McREL International
4601 DTC Boulevard, Suite 500
Denver, CO 80237 USA
Phone: 303-337-0990 • Fax: 303-337-3005
Website: www.mcrel.org • E-mail: info@mcrel.org

PAPERBACK ISBN: 978-1-4166-2088-4 ASCD product #112025   n8/15
PDF E-BOOK ISBN: 978-1-4166- 2131-7; see Books in Print for other formats.
Quantity discounts: 10–49, 10%; 50+, 15%; 1,000+, special discounts (e-mail programteam@ascd.org or call 800-933-2723, ext. 5773, or 703-575-5773). For desk copies, go to www.ascd.org/deskcopy.

Library of Congress Cataloging-in-Publication Data

Goodwin, Bryan.
  Balanced leadership for powerful learning : tools for achieving success in your school / Bryan Goodwin & Greg Cameron with Heather Hein.
    pages cm
  Includes bibliographical references.
  ISBN 978-1-4166-2088-4 (pbk. : alk. paper) 1. Educational leadership–United States. 2. School management and organization–United States. 3. School principals–United States. I. Cameron, Greg. II. Hein, Heather. III. Title.
  LB2805.G64 2015
  371.200973–dc23
                    2015021658

23 22 21 20 19 18 17 16 15   1 2 3 4 5 6 7 8 9 10 11 12

BALANCED LEADERSHIP

for

Powerful Learning

TOOLS FOR ACHIEVING SUCCESS
IN YOUR SCHOOL

List of Leadership Tools

Note: Select tools may be downloaded at http://www.ascd.org/ASCD/pdf/books/Goodwin2015forms.pdf. Use the password Goodwin2015112025 to unlock the pdf.

Acknowledgments

We would like to thank the many people who helped develop and contributed to the ideas within this book. First, our sincerest thanks to Tim Waters, McREL's former president and CEO, whose research led to the creation of Balanced Leadership. Dr. Waters cowrote the groundbreaking *School Leadership That Works* and oversaw the development of McREL's school and district leadership professional development program, which has influenced thousands of principals nationally and worldwide. We would also like to acknowledge the McREL consultants who have, over the years, worked with great dedication in the field with school leaders, helping to refine the program and developing the tools and templates you'll find in this book. These consultants and partners include Kent Davis, Tony Davis, Jim Eck, Roger Goddard, Andrew Kerr, Monette McIver, JJ Sawyer, Matt Seebaum, and Mel Sussman. We'd also like to thank Mark Stevens for his on-the-ground observations, interviews, and reporting on the profiled principals. Finally, we'd like to thank Roger Fiedler, McREL's Director of Communications and Marketing, and his team for giving direction to this project.

Introduction: Learning to Lead

If you've been around public education for any length of time, you have no doubt already encountered a broad range of leadership personalities. The public education landscape has them all:

- The Nurturer
- The Fixer
- The Executive
- The Doer
- The Idealist
- The Visionary

But what we've learned in more than a decade of working with principals of all types—in every region of the United States (and beyond), at all levels of experience—is that no one personality or style is better than another. Effective leadership isn't personality driven or a set of skills or dispositions that you either have or don't have. Rather, it's something that *all* principals can learn and do.

Research has proven that certain actions and behaviors have a positive effect on student achievement, and all principals can learn these actions and behaviors and how to implement them with efficacy. They can learn how to *establish a clear focus*, keeping the work and dialogue focused on issues that matter. They can learn how to *manage the changes*—large and small—that come with making improvements. They can learn how to *create a purposeful community* in their school, one in which all teachers and staff are invested in student outcomes and believe they can make a difference.

These three overarching responsibilities of effective school leaders—establishing a clear focus, managing change, and creating a purposeful community—as well as the specific actions and behaviors that support them, were uncovered in a sweeping analysis of research conducted by McREL and first reported in the ASCD publication *School Leadership That Works* (Marzano,

Waters, & McNulty, 2005). This research, which serves as the cornerstone of this book, has since been translated into practical guidance in the form of our Balanced Leadership professional development program and implemented by thousands of school leaders across the country and around the world. In this context, the term "balanced" refers to the delicate give and take between specific leadership actions: between directing and supporting, providing answers and asking questions, and stepping up and stepping up back—themes that we explore in Chapter 3 and are also illustrated in Figure 1.

FIGURE 1
Balancing Leadership

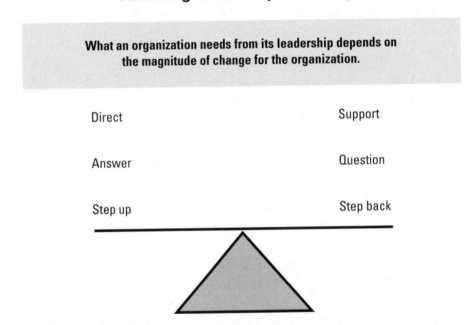

Balancing Leadership for Change

What an organization needs from its leadership depends on the magnitude of change for the organization.

Direct	Support
Answer	Question
Step up	Step back

This book captures what we've learned from these principals, synthesizing the successes and challenges they've had as they implement Balanced Leadership in their schools and districts. Our intent is to help others who know they need to and can improve, but who may not know where to start. How do you integrate the actions and behaviors on a daily basis? Which tools are most valuable? What elements will lead to the greatest change in practice?

We include stories of principals who have transformed their schools through effective leadership, as well as select tools and tips that leaders tell us have made the biggest difference. As you strive to improve your own practice and transform your own school, we hope this book will both inspire and guide you and your leadership team as you put your intentions into action.

Please note that portions of this book have been previously published in *School Leadership That Works* by Robert J. Marzano, by Timothy Waters, and Brian A. McNulty (ASCD, 2005); *The Balanced Leadership Framework* by Timothy Waters and Greg Cameron (McREL, 2007); *District Leadership That Works* by Robert J. Marzano and Timothy Waters (Solution Tree, 2009); and in various materials created by McREL for its Balanced Leadership professional development program.

CHAPTER 1

Balanced Leadership: What the Research Says

Schools in the United States have been organized around some sort of "leader" or "manager" since the early 20th century, when one-room schoolhouses transitioned to schools with multiple grades and classrooms. Teachers fulfilled this role initially, but as schools became more complex organizations, the need for full-time administrators led to the birth of the role of "principal."

The primary duties of principals have changed dramatically since then, and principals have long suspected that the many functions they fulfill, as building managers and instructional leaders, affect their schools' bottom line—student achievement. But until fairly recently, no one had proven empirically that this is the case.

The Meta-Analysis

In 2001, McREL set out to study the links between school leadership and student achievement. We undertook a meta-analysis of school-level leadership for the purpose of answering the following questions: Is there an empirical relationship between principal leadership and student achievement? If so, is the relationship positive or negative? And is it strong enough to matter to those who lead schools (principals and school-level leadership teams) and those who supervise principals?

Today, these questions seem naïve; of course there is an empirical relationship between principal leadership and student achievement. Nowadays we read frequently about the effect of high-quality leadership on achievement being second only to the effect of high-quality instruction. Before our study, however, this was an unanswered question.

The results of our meta-analysis, which were first reported in the white paper *Balanced Leadership: What 30 Years of Research Tells Us About the Effect of Leadership on Student Achievement* (Waters, Marzano, & McNulty, 2003), answered soundly the questions we had about school-level leadership.

Yes, there is an empirical relationship between leadership and student achievement.

Yes, the relationship is generally positive, though not always.

Yes, from our perspective, the average effect of leadership is strong enough to matter to principals and those who supervise them.

Specifically, we not only discovered *a positive, empirical, statistically significant relationship* between school-level leadership and student achievement, but also identified *21 specific leadership responsibilities*, along with practices that fulfill them, each with their own positive, empirical relationship to student achievement. (See Figure 1.1 for a list of the 21 leadership responsibilities and the appendix for an expanded chart that includes the associated practices and the effect sizes.)

In addition, the meta-analysis, which included 69 quantitative studies culled from more than 5,000 research studies completed during three decades, showed that we could predict that *95 percent of the time, when these responsibilities are fulfilled effectively by strong leaders, we will find higher average levels of student achievement* than we would in comparable schools where these responsibilities are not fulfilled effectively.

The Factor Analysis

Although our study asked and answered meaningful questions, answers to one set of questions led to other questions. The meta-analysis left us wanting to know more about the 21 leadership responsibilities that surfaced and our explanation for the finding that we labeled as the "differential impact of leadership," which occurred when principals were rated as strong leaders by staff and supervisors in schools with lower-than-expected student achievement. We wanted to know if there really were 21 specific leadership responsibilities, or if they were intercorrelated such that they could be reduced to a smaller number. We suspected several were intercorrelated, and the actual number of leadership responsibilities positively and empirically associated with achievement was smaller.

To answer this new set of questions, we conducted a second study, a factor analysis, which we began by developing a survey to collect data from 659 principals. We used these survey responses to factor analyze the 21 responsibilities and the relationship between the responsibilities and change associated with principals' improvement initiatives. Once again, we were surprised.

We learned that the responsibilities were *not* intercorrelated enough to warrant combining or eliminating any of them. We also discovered the importance of magnitude of change: Although all 21 responsibilities were positively correlated with first-order change (change that doesn't require a huge shift in action or perception), only 11 were correlated with second-order change

FIGURE 1.1

21 Leadership Responsibilities Positively Correlated with Student Achievement

Affirmation: Recognizes and celebrates school accomplishments and acknowledges failures

Change Agent: Is willing to challenge and actively challenges the status quo

Communication: Establishes strong lines of communication with and among teachers and students

Contingent Rewards: Recognizes and rewards individual accomplishments

Culture: Fosters shared beliefs and a sense of community and cooperation

Discipline: Protects teachers from issues and influences that would detract from their teaching time or focus

Flexibility: Adapts his or her leadership behavior to the needs of the current situation and is comfortable with dissent

Focus: Establishes clear goals and keeps those goals in the forefront of the school's attention

Ideals and Beliefs: Communicates and operates from strong ideals and beliefs about schooling

Input: Involves teachers in the design and implementation of important decisions and policies

Intellectual Stimulation: Ensures faculty and staff are aware of the most current theories and practices and makes the discussion of these a regular aspect of the school's culture

Involvement in Curriculum, Instruction, and Assessment: Is directly involved in the design and implementation of curriculum, instruction, and assessment practices

Knowledge of Curriculum, Instruction, and Assessment: Is knowledgeable about current curriculum, instruction, and assessment practices

Monitor and Evaluate: Monitors the effectiveness of school practices and their impact on student learning

Optimize: Inspires and leads new and challenging innovations

Order: Establishes a set of standard operating procedures and routines

Outreach: Is an advocate and spokesperson for the school to all stakeholders

Relationships: Demonstrates an awareness of the personal aspects of teachers and staff

Resources: Provides teachers with materials and professional development necessary for the successful execution of their jobs

Situational Awareness: Is aware of the details and undercurrents in the running of the school and uses this information to address the current and potential problems

Visibility: Has quality contact and interactions with teachers and students

(change that requires new knowledge and skills, challenges existing norms, or conflicts with personal values), and only 7 of those were positive.

Our factor analysis showed evidence that the four negatively correlated responsibilities—*Culture*, *Communication*, *Order*, and *Input*—could be explained by the concept of "implementation dip." In other words, when schools undertake initiatives requiring second-order change, these four areas tend to get worse before they get better, and a decline in performance is not uncommon.

The results of the factor analysis were, in the view of many, as meaningful as what we learned through the meta-analysis. We included all of these findings, our conclusions, and our recommendations in *School Leadership That Works: From Research to Results* (Marzano, Waters, & McNulty, 2005).

The Balanced Leadership Framework

We realized the complexity for principals in managing and implementing 21 responsibilities and their associated 66 practices. To help school leaders organize this information and connect their vision with a plan of action, we developed the Balanced Leadership Framework (see Figure 1.2), which provides a structure that connects our research findings with other relevant, research-based knowledge on school improvement, and on change and organizational management.

FIGURE 1.2

Balanced Leadership Framework

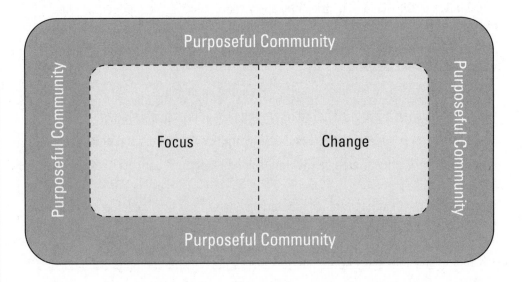

All 21 responsibilities are divided, as you will see in later chapters, among the three components, which represent, broadly, the key elements of effective school-level leadership: (1) establishing a clear focus, (2) managing change, and (3) creating a purposeful community. All 21 responsibilities are divided among these three components, which represent, broadly, the key elements of effective leadership:

Establishing a clear focus. When leaders focus on the right classroom and school practices, they can have a powerful positive effect. If they focus on practices unlikely to make a difference, however, even strong leaders can have a minimal or even negative effect on student performance.

Managing change. Even when school leaders focus on the right practices, it's imperative that they set the stage for change and understand the implications of both first- and second-order change for stakeholders—and adjust their leadership behaviors accordingly. If they don't, implementation will suffer and changes will have a minimal, if not detrimental, effect.

Creating a purposeful community. Virtually everything in a school occurs within the context of a community, composed of students, parents, teachers and other school staff members, central office staff, the school board, other social agencies, and businesses. The more this diverse community is able to coalesce around shared purposes, the more sustainable and effective a school's change efforts will be.

We believe that leaders are continually engaged in focusing the work of their schools, leading changes of different magnitudes, and developing purposeful communities. Therefore, the dotted lines of the framework, as shown in Figure 1.2, reflect permeable, rather than rigid, boundaries among the three components.

The framework also provides guidance to principals as they fulfill the 21 leadership responsibilities. Focusing the work of the school, leading change, and developing purposeful communities are *what* effective principals do; skillfully fulfilling the 21 responsibilities is *how* they do it.

Principals fulfill many and varied responsibilities that are important in running a school; however, not all of them are essential to improving student achievement. Our research findings help principals balance their time and efforts in fulfilling both important *and* essential responsibilities.

The concept of Balanced Leadership comes from a paradox we observed about the responsibilities. Some of them have the effect of stabilizing behavior and reinforcing the status quo of routines, procedures, and practices (*Culture*; *Discipline*; *Focus*; *Order*; *Involvement in Curriculum, Instruction, and Assessment*); others have the effect of destabilizing or challenging existing behaviors, which likely disrupts routines, procedures, and practices (*Change Agent*, *Flexibility*, *Ideals and Beliefs*, *Intellectual Stimulation*, *Optimize*). Balancing when and how to maintain the status quo with when and how to challenge it is often the difference between effective and ineffective leadership.

Our research findings and the Balanced Leadership Framework do not cover everything a principal needs to know and do, but they do specify the knowledge and skills that have the greatest impact on student achievement—and can help leaders balance "status quo" responsibilities with "challenge" responsibilities. (Tool #1 can help you get started in determining where to focus your attention.) We are confident that any leader, regardless of experience level or disposition, who focuses on the 21 responsibilities can improve his or her leadership and ensure high-quality experiences for every student, every day, in every classroom.

Balanced Leadership Framework Analysis

Purpose: This tool provides the opportunity for school leaders to assess the status of their school in relation to the components of the Balanced Leadership Framework. Having a better idea of the areas that need more focused attention will assist in addressing specific responsibilities associated with (1) establishing a clear focus, (2) managing change, and (3) creating a purposeful community.

Directions:
1. The questions are related to each of the three framework areas. Think about the extent to which you and your school's leadership team have taken these actions and answer on a scale of 1 to 4, with 1 representing "Not at all" and 4 representing "To a great extent."

2. In the far right column, write examples of the actions taken.

	1	2	3	4	ACTIONS
	NOT AT ALL ⟶ TO A GREAT EXTENT				
ESTABLISHING A CLEAR FOCUS TO WHAT EXTENT HAVE WE . . .					
Focused on improving research-based, school-level practices?					
Focused on improving research-based, classroom-level practices?					
Focused on influencing research-based student characteristics?					
MANAGING CHANGE TO WHAT EXTENT HAVE WE . . .					
Created tension between our current reality and our preferred future?					
Promoted understanding of the content of the change initiative and supported our staff as they put the change initiative into practice?					
Understood personal responses to the change initiative and how to manage them effectively?					
Understood the technical aspects of implementing change as well as the magnitude of the change?					
CREATING A PURPOSEFUL COMMUNITY TO WHAT EXTENT HAVE WE . . .					
Developed meaningful outcomes that we can only accomplish as a community?					
Agreed upon how we communicate, share leadership, and create a sense of order for our work?					
Identified our human, financial, symbolic, and substantive assets to accomplish our shared goals?					
Established a shared belief that we can organize and execute a course of action that makes a difference for student achievement?					

CHAPTER 2

Establishing a Clear Focus

Like any principal of a large, comprehensive urban high school, Mike Andersen's list of duties at Barry Goldwater High School (BGHS) in Phoenix is almost endless. Expectations to perform well are high. The consequences of not performing well, given the pressure of today's state and federal accountability systems, are severe.

At the very least, Principal Andersen's job requires a great deal of multi-tasking, a fair amount of political skill, the tact and touch of a thoughtful psychologist, the ability to understand and shape school budget, and the ability to do a knock-out job of appraising his team of teachers.

"When things go perfect, it's a hard job," he says. "And they rarely go perfect."

Andersen, the school's former band director, oversees a diverse student body of nearly 2,000 low- to middle-income students. Yet, rather than getting lost in an avalanche of administrative details and the often overwhelming challenges of managing a high school, Andersen has established and maintained a clear focus toward improvement.

His motivation for doing so was threefold: First, teachers at BGHS were struggling and unhappy. Second, Andersen saw students "stumbling" out of high school rather than being "launched" into life the way he imagined they should. And third, the grading system lacked integrity and produced inaccurate information about a student's capabilities.

"Our grades were haphazard, and the whole process was polluted," says Andersen. "You got points for just showing up and bringing your books every day."

Andersen started with a central question, one that he just threw out at a staff meeting without thinking it through too much: "What are grades *for*?" he asked his staff. What followed, Andersen says, was probably the most heated discussion he's ever been involved in, one that "provoked passion and emotion beyond belief."

But Andersen kept at it. He was and continues to be driven by his concern about the bigger picture: the state of public education today. He firmly believes the United States must catch up with global competition and that students should graduate from high school ready to be successful and excited about their future.

"I just kept asking [my staff] the questions over and over," says Andersen. "It wasn't personal. It was about the system. The questions were about the quality of the system we were running. The conversation was about choosing to accept the way things were or imagining a new school that was built around the right principles and then finding a way to instill those throughout everything we do."

At their core, the questions about grading and graduation went straight to the heart of the school's performance and, in some way, its soul. Andersen was holding the school's character up to a mirror.

So how did his staff answer his questions? One camp of teachers believed the grades were compensation for many things and could also recognize effort. Another camp believed grades were meant as communication to students and parents; they were a signal.

Andersen pushed to separate effort from achievement. "That was the biggie," he recalls—no more benefit of the doubt. At the same time, Andersen challenged the idea on campus that summative assessments could only be taken once. He argued that students should have multiple chances to pass the "big" tests. Andersen argued that in life you almost always get multiple opportunities—to earn your driver's license, to take college-entrance exams, to get into medical school. Even when you don't file your taxes correctly, you get another chance. So why not in school?

The teachers started to come around. Andersen focused on the "early innovators" and "early adopters" who stepped up to try the approach. Andersen made his questions the agenda for the school—and made it clear that this was his priority.

Slowly, the approach began to take hold and the tide turned. Now, grades at BGHS are not arbitrary but based solely on standards.

Getting Focused by Establishing Clear Goals

Getting and staying focused is a challenge for any school leader, whose days and weeks can be spent just ensuring the school runs smoothly, without ever focusing on student learning, improvement, or change efforts. However, a study of high-needs, high-performing, "beat-the-odds" schools conducted by McREL researchers (McREL, 2005) found that two of the key characteristics that separated these schools from their lower-performing counterparts were *academic press for achievement* (high expectations for all students) and *shared mission and goals* (a clear focus for improvement efforts and resources). In short, these top-performing schools had established and articulated clear goals for learning and then focused their energies and resources on achieving those goals.

That approach may sound obvious, but it's easy and all too common for schools to fall into a different pattern, one that makes them feel like they're running in many directions at once without a clear sense of purpose or direction. Consider the following example: Years ago, a team of researchers encountered a school where the principal—in an effort to do what she thought was best for students—had been relentless in her pursuit of every new funding opportunity and program she could find. She had sent her teachers to nearly every professional conference in the city, and filled her school with computers, books, and other tools.

The researchers likened all the activity and "stuff" to "a Christmas tree laden with ornaments" (Bryk, Sebring, Kerbow, Rollow, & Easton, 1998, p. 115). But in the end, none of the "stuff" did what it was supposed to do: raise student achievement. The efforts were fragmented and incoherent and did little to strengthen the core of the school. As a result, the teachers were consumed with activity, but not focusing on what matters most. The researchers concluded that "it was as if the branches of the tree sagged from the weight of all the ornaments, while the trunk was withering and the roots were dry" (Bryk et al., 1998, p. 115). Strong school leaders, in contrast, cut through the clutter by establishing challenging goals and performance targets, which they use to focus people on doing what matters most—and only what matters most (Public Impact, 2008).

In light of these studies and observations, it's not surprising, then, that one of the responsibilities of school leaders we found strongly correlated with student achievement was to have clear goals. Figure 2.1 shows this responsibility and the related classroom and school practices.

FIGURE 2.1

Leadership Responsibility and Practices to Focus Schools on Clear Goals

RESPONSIBILITY	CLASSROOM AND SCHOOL PRACTICES
Focus: *Establishes clear goals and keeps those goals in the forefront of the school's attention*	• Establishes high, concrete goals and expectations that all students meet those goals • Establishes high, concrete goals for curriculum, instruction, and assessment practices within the school • Establishes high, concrete goals for the general functioning of the school • Continually keeps attention on established goals

Having goals, notes one study of effective school-turnaround efforts, allows principals to focus on tactics that work and "discard tactics that do not work," engaging in a "pruning and growing process" that focuses schools on activities that have the most impact (Public Impact, 2008, p. 6). What research and experience show—and what Mike Andersen's story illustrates—is that, in practice, schools can't tackle every perceived problem at once. Principal Andersen focused on one simple question: the purpose of grades at BGHS.

Keep it simple

Zeroing in on one or two things, while straightforward in theory, is difficult in practice. Truly focusing on one or two things requires principals and school leadership teams to have the courage to put all of their eggs, so to speak, in just one or two baskets. Leaders may worry they'll be accused of not pushing for more change in their schools. They may wonder, Can I convince my superintendent that we're just going to focus on one thing this year?

As a result, many leadership teams end up drafting dizzyingly complex plans that include dozens of strategies and activities they hope to accomplish in a 180-day school year. Perhaps feeling frantic about improving achievement (or perhaps wanting to prevent second-guessing in the central office), they tend to grasp at everything they can imagine might raise performance—from student-behavior and parent-involvement programs to flipping classrooms and aligning instruction with standards. As a result, not much happens—except for exhaustion, failure, and a growing sense of hopelessness.

There's another way to think about change. Instead of doing a bunch of disparate activities in hopes that, together, they'll have some impact, we can start with one or two efforts and recognize that getting them done well will require aligning many other activities with them. Stated differently, it's important to recognize that even what seems like a simple change can have far-reaching, systemic ripple effects—as illustrated by Mike Andersen's question about the purpose of grades.

Imagine that you want to encourage your teachers to adopt new mathematics teaching practices. The proposition sounds simple, but such a change may require the school to develop and implement teacher training, coaching protocols, walk-through look-fors, model lessons, and instructional materials, not to mention having frank conversations with staff about "deprivatizing" their teaching practice. Some parents may balk at the new practices, so you'll probably need to engage your school's accountability committee in conversation and ask for parent volunteers to support the changes in the classroom. In short, even small changes can turn out to be large efforts, which is why trying to do too many things is usually a recipe for doing nothing well and winding up with little to show for it.

Knowing that schools can really only do a few things well each year also raises the stakes on making good decisions about what improvements to pursue. Indeed, as noted earlier, one of the big conclusions we drew from our findings about the differential impact of school leaders—that is, that some principals whose teachers saw them as strong leaders could still wind up with flat achievement—was that they may be focusing their schools on doing the *wrong* things.

Focus on what matters most

So where to begin? School leaders can turn to research to ensure their improvement efforts are focused on the right things. An analysis of thousands of research studies, reported in *Simply Better: Doing What Matters Most to Change the Odds for Student Success* (Goodwin, 2011b), offers an effective way to focus school improvement on the changes that matter most. It identifies five key leverage points that research suggests, when addressed well, can lead to dramatic gains in student achievement:

- **Guarantee challenging, engaging, and intentional instruction.** At the core of effective systems are teachers who challenge students, develop positive relationships with them, and are intentional in their use of a broad repertoire of teaching strategies.

- **Ensure curricular pathways to success.** High-performing systems guarantee that all students, in every classroom, no matter what their aspirations, are provided with both *challenging* and *personalized* learning experiences that prepare each of them for life success.

- **Provide whole-child student supports.** To help students meet high expectations, school systems need to provide cognitive, emotional, and learning supports to address a variety of student-level factors that are crucial to their success, such as home environment, background knowledge, and motivation.

- **Create high-performance school cultures.** Effective schools ensure high-quality learning experiences in every classroom. At the same time, they develop a culture of high expectations for learning and behavior, which is an even more powerful predictor of student success than socioeconomic status.

- **Develop data-driven, high-reliability systems.** High-performing school systems put data systems and processes in place to ensure high-quality learning experiences for all students and follow established procedures for providing real-time responses to student failures. (Goodwin, 2011b, pp. 5–7)

All five components of what we call the What Matters Most framework are critical; however, few, if any, examples exist of schools or districts that have succeeded in improving all five components *at once*. That's not to say that continuous improvement efforts shouldn't eventually address several or all of the components, but doing something right requires a more limited approach. As noted earlier, most school improvement endeavors require more time and effort than initially expected.

Find the right focus for your school

A variety of strategies, processes, and tools are available to determine the right focus for your school. Tool #2 (see page 19) is designed to help keep improvement efforts focused and manageable by pinpointing which of the five areas is most critical for you and your leadership team to be working on right now.

The tool is a form of root-cause analysis, which is a practice to solve problems by attempting to identify and correct the root causes of events, as opposed to simply addressing their symptoms. The tool employs a process that we have found useful for school leaders: the Five Whys, or Why-Because. The technique is quite simple—as you've probably witnessed if you're a parent. Despite the hair-pulling frustration this technique may cause when used by a young child, the Five Whys has been demonstrated to be a credible method of problem solving.

One of the best-known examples of the Five Whys is the story of the deteriorating memorial in Washington, D.C. Although there are differing versions, with varying embellishments, the story is essentially this: A group of private consultants was hired by the United States Park Service to study the deterioration of the Jefferson Memorial and the Lincoln Memorial (Gross, 2014). Using the Five Whys process, the consultants asked these questions:

Why #1—Why is the [Jefferson or Lincoln] monument deteriorating?
- Because harsh chemicals are frequently used to clean the monument.

Why #2—Why are harsh chemicals needed?
- To clean off the large number of bird droppings on the monument.

Why #3—Why are there a large number of bird droppings on the monument?
- Because the large population of spiders in and around the monument are a food source to the local birds.

Why #4—Why is there a large population of spiders in and around the monument?
- Because vast swarms of insects, on which the spiders feed, are drawn to the monument at dusk.

Why #5—Why are swarms of insects drawn to the monument at dusk?
- Because the lighting of the monument in the evening attracts the local insects. (Gross, 2014)

Hence, the consultants arrived at the solution: Change how and when the monument is illuminated in the evening to prevent attracting the swarming insects. If the consultants had not used repeated cycles of Why-Because, their solution may have been much more drastic and expensive than changing the timing of the lighting of the monuments to later in the evening—and the solution would have most likely been ineffective.

The story illustrates the need for a thorough understanding of cause and effect before acting too hastily on a perceived solution. There is nothing especially magical in asking why five times, other than it pushes you to dig deeper into the root cause of the problem rather than just stopping at a superficial solution.

This memorial story has an interesting side note: A pilot program to turn the lights on later in the evening proved to be effective, but complaints from photographers about losing the scene of a brightly illuminated monument against the backdrop of a colorful sunset prompted the Park Service to abandon this solution and try various other measures, purportedly with much more limited success (Gross, 2014). This story illustrates two key cautions when conducting root-cause analysis. The first is the importance of clear problem identification: If we are not clear and precise in defining the problem we are trying to solve, we may end up with the right solution, but for the wrong problem. A second caution lies in the perils of identifying only *one* causal factor, when, in fact, you may be dealing with complex structures with many interrelated factors—which suggests you may need to explore problem solving from more of a systemic mindset, identifying multiple contributing factors (with, potentially, different root causes for each) and determining which one or two of those to take action on first. In Tool #2, we show how using the What Matters Most framework with the Five Whys might help to identify instructional, curricular, student support, school culture, and organizational process issues that are contributing to a single identified problem.

Identify outcomes and a goal

Now that you've identified the root causes of the problem, it's time to switch your thinking from "glass half empty" problem identification to "glass half full" visualization of a more ideal state for your school. Tool #3 (p. 20) is designed to help you and your school leadership team identify your desired outcomes as a clear and measurable goal.

Combining the Five Whys and the What Matters Most Framework

Purpose: This tool is designed to help keep improvement efforts focused and manageable by helping you and your leadership team determine which of the five areas in the What Matters Most framework is the best starting point.

Directions:

1. State a problem you wish to address and decide which element of the What Matters Most framework best explains the situation.

2. Continue to ask "why" and choose an explanatory factor a total of five times. The framework element you have identified at the end is the one you may want to focus on now. (You'll find a completed example at the end of the tool.)

What is the problem? _____

1. Why is that occurring?

This is an issue related to ☐ Instruction ☐ Curriculum ☐ Student engagement/supports ☐ School culture ☐ Organizational processes/ focus/data use

2. Why is that occurring?

This is an issue related to ☐ Instruction ☐ Curriculum ☐ Student engagement/supports ☐ School culture ☐ Organizational processes/ focus/data use

3. Why is that occurring?

This is an issue related to ☐ Instruction ☐ Curriculum ☐ Student engagement/supports ☐ School culture ☐ Organizational processes/ focus/data use

4. Why is that occurring?

This is an issue related to ☐ Instruction ☐ Curriculum ☐ Student engagement/supports ☐ School culture ☐ Organizational processes/ focus/data use

5. Why is that occurring?

This is an issue related to ☐ Instruction ☐ Curriculum ☐ Student engagement/supports ☐ School culture ☐ Organizational processes/ focus/data use

Example

What is the problem? Student reading scores slump in 4th grade.

1. Why is that occurring? As students begin reading in the content areas (transitioning from learning to read to reading to learn), they struggle to keep up.

This is an issue related to ☐ Instruction ☑ Curriculum ☐ Student Engagement/supports ☐ School culture ☐ Organizational processes/ focus/data use

2. Why is that occurring? Students lack the vocabulary they need to comprehend the content area material.

This is an issue related to ☐ Instruction ☐ Curriculum ☑ Student engagement/supports ☐ School culture ☐ Organizational processes/ focus/data use

3. Why is that occurring? Students do not read enough nonfiction in earlier grades.

This is an issue related to ☑ Instruction ☐ Curriculum ☐ Student engagement/supports ☐ School culture ☐ Organizational processes/ focus/data use

4. Why is that occurring? We haven't articulated the need for nonfiction reading in early grades.

This is an issue related to ☐ Instruction ☐ Curriculum ☐ Student engagement/supports ☐ School culture ☑ Organizational processes/ focus/data use

5. Why is that occurring? K–2 and 3–5 teachers are siloed and don't work together on vertical alignment of curriculum.

This is an issue related to ☐ Instruction ☐ Curriculum ☐ Student engagement/supports ☑ School culture ☐ Organizational processes/ focus/data use

Identifying and Specifying Desired Outcomes

Purpose: This tool is designed to help school leaders identify desired outcomes and restate them as clear and measurable goals.

Directions:

1. **Reflect** upon your completed Five Whys and What Matters Most worksheet (Tool #2). You should be able to select a student outcome, stated in quantifiable terms, that requires important changes to current practices.

2. **Identify who will benefit.** Focus on who will benefit from your efforts. Here, there's a natural tendency to say that all students in your school will benefit from your efforts. However, goal setting requires making strategic decisions about where to focus your energies; focusing everywhere at once is no focus at all. Certainly, your school should remain committed to teaching all students, but your improvement efforts should target those students most in need of attention and intervention (e.g., the 25 percent of grade 4–5 students not proficient in reading comprehension).

3. **By how much.** Once you've identified this population, set a goal that strikes a balance between being achievable and sending a signal that the status quo will no longer be tolerated and that multiple changes will be required to reach the goal.

4. **By when.** Finally, affix a time-bound element to your goals to create a sense of urgency that will help keep your entire leadership team and everyone in your school focused on achieving the goal (e.g., "Remember, we need to stay on track to make these improvements by December").

BY WHEN

- Use time-bound goals to create a sense of urgency.

- Use time-bound measures to keep everyone on track and accountable.

BY HOW MUCH

- Make it clear that the status quo is no longer acceptable.

- Set a stretch goal that requires a concerted effort of many people (e.g., more than a simple fix) to achieve.

IDENTIFY WHO WILL BENEFIT

- Be specific, clarifying the target population for your initiative.

Your Highest Priority:
Ensuring Consistent, High-Quality Teaching

Although systems thinking is important and we advise school leadership teams to consider multiple root causes for the challenges they see, it's worth noting that research on schools and successful turnaround efforts suggests that, typically, the biggest opportunity for improving student achievement lies in improving the consistency of instruction. Indeed, one of the largest studies of classrooms ever conducted—a compilation of surveys and achievement data for more than 54,000 students over 30 years—found "considerable teacher heterogeneity" in the sample (Konstantopoulos, 2005) and that variances in teaching quality accounted for more of the differences in student achievement (in some cases, twice as much) than variances in school quality.

Stated differently, in any school, you're likely to find exemplary teachers, mediocre teachers, and teachers who need significant support to improve their practices. As a result, the quality of students' learning experiences is largely left to chance—namely, the teacher to which they are assigned. Reducing the variability in teaching quality—and ensuring that no matter what classroom students are in, they'll encounter productive, supportive learning environments—is often the single most important way to improve school performance. This conclusion suggests that a school leadership team's efforts should focus on guaranteeing high-quality instruction across the entire school. Indeed, we might think of this as the highest priority for principals and school leadership teams. Not surprisingly, in our meta-analysis of research on effective school leaders, three of the key leadership responsibilities we identified have a particularly strong link to improving instructional quality, as shown in Figure 2.2.

Be an instructional leader

A study that followed our meta-analysis solidifies this point. A team of researchers (Robinson, Lloyd, & Rowe, 2008) conducted two additional meta-analyses of research on school leadership to parse out the effect of what they identified as two distinctly different leadership styles: *instructional leadership* (i.e., behaviors focused on teacher development, including setting high expectations for students, articulating clear learning and teaching objectives, and creating learning environments free from disruptions) and *transformational leadership* (i.e., behaviors focused on organizational development, including creating a shared vision for success, inspiring staff, and bringing moral purpose to schooling). The differences in effect size between these two leadership styles were striking: Behaviors that focused directly on teacher development were found to have effect sizes three to four times greater than those for behaviors focused on organizational development.

FIGURE 2.2

Leadership Responsibilities and Practices That Focus on Teaching and Learning

RESPONSIBILITIES	CLASSROOM AND SCHOOL PRACTICES
Resources: *Provides teachers with the materials and professional development necessary for the successful execution of their jobs*	• Ensures that teachers and staff have the necessary materials and equipment • Ensures that teachers and staff have the necessary professional development opportunities that directly enhance their teaching
Involvement in Curriculum, Instruction, and Assessment: *Is directly involved in the design and implementation of curriculum, instruction, and assessment practices*	• Is directly involved in helping teachers design curricular activities and address assessment and instructional issues
Discipline: *Protects teachers from issues and influences that would detract from their teaching time or focus*	• Protects instructional time from interruptions • Protects/shelters teachers and staff from internal and external distractions

The researchers cautioned that this doesn't necessarily mean *transformational* leadership is unimportant; indeed, in some schools, they noted, focusing on such things as "orderliness, safety, and civility may be an essential prior stage before leaders can give more attention to the curriculum and teacher professional learning" (Robinson, Lloyd, & Rowe, 2008, p. 668). Nonetheless, the study makes clear that the biggest opportunities for principals and school leadership teams to positively influence student achievement likely lie in visiting classrooms, observing teaching, coaching teachers to higher levels of performance, evaluating their performance against high expectations for teaching, and supporting their ongoing professional growth.

Keep the focus on curriculum and instruction

Author and school improvement expert Mike Schmoker (2011) has written that getting curriculum and instruction right in a school is often the equivalent to a football team getting the basics of blocking and tackling down before moving on to anything else. Schmoker, a former football coach himself, notes that when a team is losing, a coach's tendency can be to throw out the old playbook and draw up new plays. The only trouble is, unless the team gets better at the fundamentals, they are likely to execute the new plays just as poorly as the old ones, and so the losing streak continues. Schools that fail to address the core fundamentals of good instruction and to faithfully enact curriculum are likely to suffer the same fate: a lot of change but few results, or, to paraphrase Shakespeare, much sound and fury, signifying nothing.

It's no coincidence, then, that two of the responsibilities of effective leaders we discovered through our original meta-analysis were *Involvement in Curriculum, Instruction, and Assessment*, and *Resources*, both of which relate to ensuring that teachers have the resources and professional development needed to improve their instructional practices. Nor is it any coincidence that the leaders we observed focused most of their time and energy—and improvement plans—on ensuring that these basics were in place; for example, by constantly talking with teachers about good instruction, reviewing assessment and grading practices, and becoming deeply involved in how teachers were making the curriculum come alive in their classrooms.

Let teachers teach

Although the statement "Let teachers teach" may seem obvious, the reality in many schools is that a great deal of instructional time is lost to distractions such as announcements, assemblies, and "administrivia" tasks like dealing with parental permission forms. Indeed, over the past few decades, researchers have consistently identified time for learning as one of the strongest correlates of student success. A synthesis of 3,000 studies (Walberg, 1984) found that time spent on instruction had a correlation of 0.38—which is not only statistically significant, but also much greater than the link between student socioeconomic status and achievement (0.25). And yet researchers have found that large proportions of time students spend in school are *not* devoted to instruction or learning. The National Center for Education Statistics (1997), for example, examined data from 53,008 elementary teachers and found that on average, teachers spent only about 68 percent of school time teaching core academic curriculum. The rest of their time appears to have been devoted to other nonacademic activities, such as recess, lunch, noncore subjects, and classroom management. Lack of time to teach remains a problem for teachers nationwide; with the increased focus on high-stakes testing, teachers are also expected to squeeze in test prep. A study of teachers in Washington found that, although teachers report spending 72 percent of their time on direct instruction, 15 to 17.8 percent of that time was devoted to preparing students for state tests (Central Washington University, 2014).

In our own meta-analysis of leadership research, we found that the extent to which leaders were able to protect time for learning from external distractions—a responsibility we call *Discipline*—was strongly correlated with student achievement. What this finding means is that leaders and their leadership teams ought to view learning time as sacred and find ways to stamp out activities that disrupt learning. As teachers will readily tell you, even something as seemingly benign as a PA announcement can disrupt valuable classroom learning time, derailing classroom conversations and teachable moments.

Staying Focused: Finishing What We Start

One of the biggest challenges for schools isn't starting a new initiative; it's finishing what they start. As Harvard researcher Richard Elmore (2002) has observed, "Schools are accustomed to changing—promiscuously and routinely—without producing any improvement" (p. 13). Staying focused long enough to see change bear fruit, it seems, is a much more difficult enterprise. From 2009 until 2011 the U.S. Department of Education's Institute for Education Sciences sponsored more than two dozen scientific studies of well-known programs to determine which ones had a positive effect on student achievement. In the end, only *one* study found any positive results of the well-regarded programs they examined. Yet over and over again, implementation was so poor it was hard to determine whether the program—or application of the program—was at fault (Goodwin, 2011a). For example, in a study of Thinking Reader software, use dropped off so much that, by the end of the school year, only 8.9 percent of students had finished the third and final novel supported by the software (Drummond et al., 2011). At issue may have been a number of factors, including poor teacher buy-in, but also a lack of leadership follow-through. For example, in the study of Project CRISS, a pedagogical approach designed to encourage students to have greater engagement in and ownership of their learning, only 3 of the 23 leadership teams organized the required number of teacher study-group meetings; only two-thirds of the principals conducted required classroom walk-throughs to monitor program adoption (Kushman, Hanita, & Raphael, 2011). What this finding suggests is that when a school fails to properly implement a new initiative, ultimately the school leader and leadership team are at fault.

Shrink the change with "fractal experiences"

One key to getting a job done is making sure it's actually doable. In their book *Switch: How to Change Things When Change Is Hard*, Chip and Dan Heath (2010) describe the importance of "shrinking the change"—whether it's getting out of debt by paying off your smallest balances first or cleaning your house by spending just five minutes in a single room. In our own work with schools, we encourage them to engage in what we call a "fractal experience," a small-scale, short-term effort that results in quick, measurable gains in achievement. The term *fractal* is drawn from a phenomenon found throughout nature in such things as ferns, snowflakes, and river networks—where the smallest component of the system resembles the larger system.

Schools can adopt small-scale, carefully designed school improvement experiences that contain the same elements as a larger schoolwide improvement effort (such as using data, setting goals, clarifying individual behaviors, and monitoring implementation). For instance, we often find that underperforming schools lack a consistent approach for instruction, such as the one shown in Figure 2.3. This particular framework (Dean, Hubbell, Pitler, & Stone, 2012) uses three broad components—Creating the Environment for Learning, Helping Students Develop Understanding, and Helping Students Extend and Apply Knowledge—to organize nine strategies related to effective instruction:

1. Setting Objectives and Providing Feedback
2. Reinforcing Effort and Providing Recognition
3. Cooperative Learning
4. Cues, Questions, and Advance Organizers
5. Nonlinguistic Representation
6. Summarizing and Note Taking
7. Assigning Homework and Providing Practice
8. Identifying Similarities and Differences
9. Generating and Testing Hypotheses (Dean et al., 2012, p. xviii)

Instead of recommending that all teachers perfect their delivery of all nine strategies for effective instruction at once, we encourage teachers to adopt one strategy, such as setting objectives, with consistency and fidelity. Learning how to work together as peer coaches to implement one piece with fidelity not only ensures that one strategy is being performed well in every classroom, but also creates something else: a sense of collective efficacy, or a belief among teachers that, by working together, they can improve student outcomes. We'll discuss this important concept more in subsequent chapters.

Here's an important twist on shrinking the change you may wish to try in your school: Instead of telling all teachers in the school that they must improve on the *same* strategy (which could be insulting to those who have already mastered it), encourage small groups of teachers (we recommend triads) to identify which of the nine categories of instruction they would most like to challenge themselves to improve and then work together as peer coaches in short cycles (for example, six-week periods) to help one another improve in that area.

Be clear and concrete

It's important that, from the outset, everyone is clear about what the expected new behaviors will look like. Whether you articulate these expectations in a directive way or generate them through a more collaborative process (we'll discuss the pros and cons of both approaches in Chapter 3 on

FIGURE 2.3

Framework for Instructional Planning

Creating the Environment for Learning

Setting Objectives and Providing Feedback

Reinforcing Effort and Providing Recognition

Cooperative Learning

Helping Students Develop Understanding

Cues, Questions, and Advance Organizers

Nonlinguistic Representations

Summarizing and Note Taking

Assigning Homework and Providing Practice

Helping Students Extend and Apply Knowledge

Identifying Similarities and Differences

Generating and Testing Hypotheses

Source: From *Classroom Instruction That Works* (2nd ed., p. xvi), by C. B. Dean, E. R. Hubbell, H. Pitler, and B. Stone, 2012, Alexandria, VA: ASCD. Copyright © 2012 by McREL.

managing change), it's important to articulate them so that people can begin to visualize what will be different going forward. In *Switch,* Heath and Heath call out the importance of "script[ing] the critical moves" (2010, p. 49). As they note, "What looks like resistance is often a lack of clarity" (p. 53). For example, when two professors reframed an abstract "eat healthy" campaign in West Virginia as a simple step—buying 1 percent instead of whole milk— what seemed like resistance melted away and spawned dramatic changes in behavior in two communities.

Sometimes leaders may worry that the more they prescribe behaviors, the more resistance they'll encounter, so they speak in generalities about a change and assume people will prefer to fill in the gaps and make meaning for themselves. As it turns out, though, ambiguity is exhausting. It creates what psychologists call "cognitive load" and the related phenomenon of decision paralysis—as researchers found when they invited supermarket shoppers to select from a display of 6 different types of jam versus 30; overwhelmingly, shoppers were more apt to purchase jam from the display with just 6 choices (Iyengar & Lepper, 2000).

Thus, it's important that once you've identified your goals, conducted your root-cause analysis, and identified actions to take, you translate those lofty goals and aspirations into concrete behaviors to remove ambiguity and help everyone be clear about what, exactly, will be different going forward, including what differences others will observe. As Heath and Heath put it, "ambiguity is the enemy" when it comes to change (2010, p. 53). Figure 2.4 provides some examples of how to take abstract goals and make them clearer, more concrete, and measureable.

FIGURE 2.4

Making Improvement Activities Concrete and Measureable

VAGUE	MORE SPECIFIC	MORE CONCRETE	CONCRETE PLUS MEASURES
We'll improve our use of instructional time.	We'll use bell-ringer activities when students enter class-rooms.	At the start of each class period, teachers will provide students with challenging, learning-related assignments they will be expected to complete within the first five minutes of class. Here are seven examples of bell-ringer activities.	We'll observe 100% of classrooms using bell-ringer activities at the start of the class period and 100% of students working on their bell-ringer assignments.
We'll encourage all students to participate in classroom discus-sions.	We'll use longer wait times in all classroom discussions.	We'll use three-plus seconds for Wait Time I (after teacher questions) and Wait Time II (after student responses) in all class-room discussions.	We'll observe three-plus-seconds of Wait Time after Wait Times I and II, and participa-tion of three or more students in discussions during a three-minute period.

Aim for quick wins

Research on effective school-turnaround leaders has found that a common theme among them is the tendency to focus their schools on high-priority problems that can be fixed quickly—usually within a matter of months, if not weeks (Public Impact, 2008). The most effective turnaround leaders concentrate their energies "on big, fast payoffs in year one" in order to "silence critics with speedy success" (Public Impact, 2008, p. 6). In contrast, unsuccessful improvement efforts often start with a bang and end in a whimper when those implementing the changes become unconvinced the efforts will pay off or lose faith when the efforts fail to bear fruit.

Fractal experiences make it easier for stakeholders to connect the dots between actions taken and outcomes produced. A fractal experience shrinks the change into a small-scale, quick-win effort can also help schools and school leadership teams overcome "analysis paralysis" by identifying a small change, testing it to closely monitor the effects of the change (often in six-week or 90-day cycles), and make adjustments as necessary in an iterative manner. Driving improvement through fractal experiences unburdens school leadership teams of needing to be brilliant diagnosticians of a problem or the world's most clever strategists; instead, they simply need to be willing to try something new, test its effects, and make course corrections as necessary. This shift in mindset can help to replace fear of failure with a philosophy of "fail quickly to learn quickly" or "fail forward."

Engage stakeholders and secure broad buy-in

One surefire way an improvement initiative will come off the rails is by encountering vocal opposition from the broader community, whether it be parents or central office administrators. Indeed, parents can often provide you and your leadership team with a vital, unvarnished perspective on what's happening in your school. Moreover, they can be a tremendous resource (or what we'll describe in Chapter 4 as an intangible asset) in the form of supporting teachers in the classroom, supporting student learning at home, and influencing bus stop conversations and people's perceptions of your school. If you ignore parents and other stakeholders, you do so at your own peril.

Parents can also provide you with an effective sounding board for your initiatives. If you and the members of your leadership team cannot, for example, explain to parents and central office administrators what you're doing or persuade them of the merit of your efforts, you may need to rethink some or all elements of your plan. If you can't explain in simple terms where you're going as a school, it will be difficult for those who need to implement change to understand and internalize it. Making your plan accessible to all stakeholders can be a helpful exercise in and of itself as it requires you to double-check, clarify, and sharpen your thinking. Specifically, you should be able to do the following:

- Describe the outcomes you want for students in your school.
- Articulate the *why* behind the effort—why this is important and the right thing to do.
- Specify, in concrete terms, what changes will become evident in your school and by when.
- Get feedback on your plan and revise it accordingly.

Finally, knowing how easy it is for urgent demands to distract us all from what's really important, consider how you might enlist your parent groups and central office administrators as allies in keeping you focused on your desired outcomes. If you commit to share regular reports of progress with them, you can create important milestones for tracking and reporting progress. In turn, that commitment will help to keep everyone in your school focused on executing well the changes you've identified for your school— even as inevitable side dramas and distractions emerge.

Leadership Responsibilities for Staying Focused

Three of the leadership responsibilities tied to higher student achievement that we identified in our meta-analysis of research on effective school leaders (Marzano, Waters, & McNulty, 2005) relate to helping a school sustain its focus and finish what it starts (see Figure 2.5). The first involves making sure everyone is clear about what's expected of them and the consequences for not measuring up to these expectations—a responsibility we call *Order*, which includes establishing clear (and often new) procedures and routines and being clear that changes are mandatory, not optional (Public Impact, 2008). According to studies of effective turnaround leaders, this can mean removing staff—often senior staff—who are unwilling to make the changes others are making. Doing so sends a clear message to everyone—and often a positive one to those who are working hard to change—that collegiality and professionalism are expected and staff will be rewarded for effort and quality of performance, a leadership responsibility we call *Contingent Rewards*. Finally, as noted in the previous section, effective leaders know how to engage their parents in school improvement efforts. Not surprisingly, then, one of the key correlates of effective leaders that we found in our original meta-analysis is a responsibility we label as *Outreach*, which includes ensuring that parents are generally involved in the school and its improvement efforts, and leveraging them as advocates for your school and supporters of your efforts, including as classroom and accountability resources.

Putting It All Together: A Three-Pronged Approach to Improvement

Now that you've identified the root causes of underperformance, set forth clear, measureable goals for student outcomes, and considered how to shrink the change and be concrete about action steps, it's time to pull it all together into a set of well-defined interventions—what we might call a bundle of improvement efforts.

FIGURE 2.5

Leadership Responsibilities and Practices to Sustain Focus

RESPONSIBILITIES	CLASSROOM AND SCHOOL PRACTICES
Order: *Establishes a set of standard operating procedures and routines*	• Provides and reinforces clear structures, rules, and procedures for teachers and staff • Provides and reinforces clear structures, rules, and procedures for students • Establishes routines for the effective running of the school that teachers and staff understand and follow
Contingent Rewards: *Recognizes and rewards individual accomplishments*	• Uses performance versus seniority as the primary criterion for rewards and recognition • Uses hard work and results as the basis for reward and recognition • Recognizes individuals who excel
Outreach: *Is an advocate and spokesperson for the school with all stakeholders*	• Ensures the school complies with all district and state mandates • Is an advocate of the school with the community at large • Is an advocate of the school with parents • Is an advocate of the school with central office

An improvement bundle is a concept borrowed from the Institute for Healthcare Improvement (IHI), which has found that in hospital settings, dramatic improvements can be driven by meticulously implementing a "small set of evidence-based interventions," usually three to five components that work together to yield a desired outcome (Resar, Griffin, Haraden, & Nolan, 2012, p. 1). For example, one such bundle that IHI helped hospital teams implement in order to reduce infections at intravenous (IV) sites included proper hand washing, sterilization of the skin around the IV, optimal site selection for the line, daily checks of the IV line, and removal of unnecessary lines.

So what would an intervention bundle look like in school settings? Here, we turn again to research on effective schools and school improvement efforts (Bryk, Sebring, Allensworth, Luppescu, & Easton, 2010; Marzano, 2000; Public Impact, 2008). As shown in Figure 2.6, successful improvement efforts appear to consistently focus on improvements in what we've distilled as three key interrelated areas—focus on the core, alter the student experience, and reshape the culture—that together reflect the What Matters Most framework.

You can use Tool #4 (p. 32) and Tool #5 (pp. 33–34) to put this research to work for your school. They can help you to develop your own intervention bundle and then to plan the necessary support activities.

FIGURE 2.6

Key Areas of School Improvement Focus

KEY AREAS	EXAMPLES OF IMPROVEMENT PRACTICES
Focus on the core. At the heart of most successful school improvement efforts is an explicit focus on curriculum and instruction—guaranteeing challenging, engaging, and intentional instruction and providing all students with curricular pathways to success. Indeed, it's difficult to imagine improvement efforts that do not, in some way, address teaching and learning being successful.	**Guaranteeing challenging, engaging, and intentional instruction** • Ensuring universal use of student learning objectives • Using formative assessment to guide instruction • Providing rubrics for all major assignments • Improving student summarizing and note-taking abilities **Ensuring curricular pathways to success** • Developing and using curriculum pacing guides • Improving vertical alignment through curriculum mapping • Developing engaging project-based learning opportunities • Teaching through cross-curricular assignments and projects
Alter the student experience. Research shows that student-level factors, including motivation, prior knowledge, and home environments, are powerful influences on success. Thus, improvement plans should consider what will be different for students as a result—what new supports will be in place for them and what will feel different about the learning environment to motivate them to believe they can rise to the challenge of high expectations.	**Providing whole-child student supports** • Securing strong parental and community involvement in learning • Providing out-of-school-time supports to address gaps in background knowledge • Using out-of-school activities to motivate students with engaging enrichment opportunities (e.g., robotics clubs) • Supporting student motivation with consistent messages about "growth mindsets" • Using counselors to provide students with social-emotional supports for learning • Creating learning environments that encourage student curiosity and risk taking
Reshape the culture. Typically, existing organizational norms (for students and adults) are behind low performance or performance plateaus. Improvement efforts, almost by definition, require confronting these counterproductive norms and behaviors and creating new expectations and agreed-upon processes for how people will work with one another, analyze and use data, and interact with students.	**Creating high-performance school cultures** • Establishing new norms for student behavior • Consistently conveying a strong press for achievement • Encouraging teacher collaboration with lesson planning • Deprivatizing teacher practice with walk-throughs, instructional coaches, or peer coaching • Creating "data walls" and setting expectations for ongoing data analysis • Refocusing faculty meetings on student learning • Clarifying expectations for all staff to change and to support improvement efforts, and to grow as professionals

Note: Although developing data-driven, high-reliability systems is one of the five components of the What Matters Most framework, we did not include it here because it relates to district-level leadership, not school-level leadership.

Designing an Intervention Bundle

Purpose: This tool is designed to help school leaders integrate the guidance from Figure 2.6 (p. 31) with the rubric provided in Figure 2.4 (p. 27) to create an intervention bundle that addresses key areas of school improvement by identifying concrete actions they want people to take and the measures they will use to track progress.

Directions:
1. Insert your desired outcome in the first column.
2. Fill in the specific activities, actions, and improvement measures you will undertake to achieve the outcome. Although it may be tempting to identify many changes, discipline yourself to "shrink the change" and identify just one or two in each area that you believe will matter most to achieve your student outcome. You should identify three to five specific changes each for Key Improvement Activities, Concrete Actions, and Improvement Measures to make up your intervention bundle.

DESIRED OUTCOME	KEY IMPROVEMENT ACTIVITIES	CONCRETE ACTIONS	IMPROVEMENT MEASURES
Insert the desired outcome from Leadership Tool #3 here *Within three years, 90% of 4th and 5th graders will be proficient+ in reading comprehension.*	Focus on the core (Classroom Practices) *Teach academic vocabulary to students in grades 4 and 5.*	Specify concrete changes in instruction and curriculum *Grade-level teacher teams will identify and teach academic vocabulary in each unit.*	What measures will we use to track changes in instruction and curriculum? *90% of peer observations will find academic vocabulary posted in class and students aware of key terms.*
	Alter the student experience (Student Supports) *Launch schoolwide nonfiction reading initiative, including book buddies.*	Specify new student supports *Book buddies will share weekly progress on reading 40 minutes per day.*	What measures will we use to track changes in student supports and engagement? *The number of students reading 40 minutes or more per day will increase 25%–50% in 3 months.*
	Reshape the culture (School Practices) *Use vertical planning triads to align reading curriculum.*	Specify new processes and expectations *Vertical triads will meet once every 4 weeks to develop new book buddy projects linked to academic vocabulary.*	What measures will we use to track changes in organizational norms, culture, and climate? *Triads will deliver action research project reports at faculty meetings.*

Trilateral Planning

Purpose: To help school leadership teams consider how they will support the intervention bundles identified in Tool #4, we have designed a trilateral planning tool. This tool is designed to help leadership teams identify the classroom practices, student supports, and school practices that they hope to change, along with the leadership responsibilities they and their principals will need to fulfill to successfully guide those approaches.

Directions:

1. In the middle of the inverted triangle, place the desired outcome statement you created in Leadership Tool #3 (your targeted, time-bound, stretch goal).

2. Write the Key Improvement Activities identified in Leadership Tool #4 in the three shaded areas of the largest triangle.

3. Next, identify the leadership responsibilities (see the Appendix) your team will emphasize to focus on improving teaching practices, supporting students, and changing school culture and norms. Write these adjacent to the Leadership Responsibility circles. (Note: You can select from any of the 21 responsibilities.)

4. Once you've done this, consider the following questions:

   • Do the leadership responsibilities you selected support your identified student outcome?

   • How will you specifically and intentionally emphasize these leadership responsibilities?

5. Finally, we have found that this process is most effective when you ask peers—for example, a leadership team from another school—to review your plan. You should be able to discuss your plan through these four lenses:

   • What will we do?

   • How will we do it?

   • When, exactly, will we do it?

   • Why will we do it?

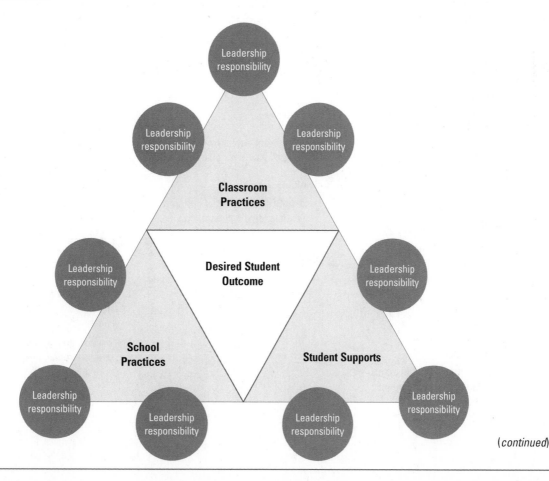

(*continued*)

Trilateral Planning

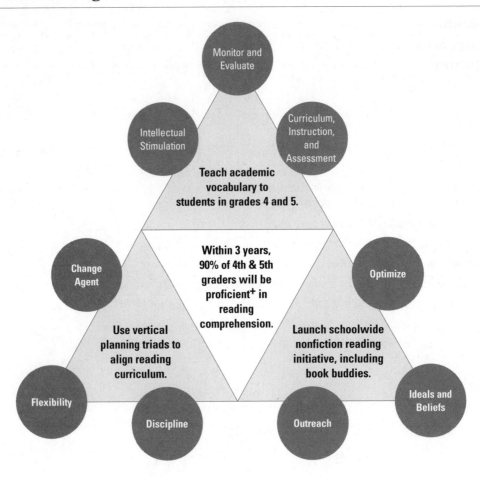

Monitor and Evaluate
- Add vocabulary activities to adapted walk-through template.
- Check for fidelity and consistency of implementation through walk-throughs and observations.

Intellectual Stimulation
- Ensure PD opportunities that focus on implementing high-quality vocabulary strategies with fidelity.

Curriculum, Instruction, and Assessment
- Meet with grade-level teams to identify specific academic vocabulary to teach.

Change Agent
- Use current achievement data to create demand for change.

Flexibility
- Identify a pilot window during which leading indicator data are collected.

Discipline
- Establish nonnegotiable reading block in schedule.

Optimize
- Ask five students, "What are you reading?" every day.

Ideals and Beliefs
- Schedule book buddy time to model reading and learning.

Outreach
- Communicate about schoolwide reading initiative to parents and families through the website, newsletters, and parent and family meetings.
- Encourage parents and families to share reading experiences with their children.

Snapshot: Barry Goldwater High School

Back in 2006, when Mike Andersen first assumed the principalship at Barry Goldwater High School, the future of the school was uncertain. Nor would many have predicted that Andersen, who is polite and pragmatic but doesn't ooze charisma, was the right person to lead a staff of about 100 teachers on a journey of transformation that would lift the school out of complacency to national recognition for its beat-the-odds performance.

Andersen himself wasn't always certain he had what it took to be an effective leader. But then one day in 2007, when he learned about the Balanced Leadership research at a workshop, something clicked. "One key piece that I learned," he recalled later, "you don't attack the people. Too often, we do that like a knee-jerk reaction. But if something's not working, it's a systemic issue. Nine times out of 10. Or 10 times out of 10."

The grading system was a perfect example: "It wasn't personal. It was about the system. The questions were about the quality of the system we were running. The conversation was about choosing to accept the way things were or imagining a new school that was built around the right principles and then finding a way to instill those throughout everything we do."

Andersen brought discipline to the school. Staff development days became "sacred"; the expectation is that everyone will be there, and attendance is taken. More than anything else, though, Andersen took up the mantle of being the person in the school who continues to ask tough questions about those systems and keep everyone pressing ahead—pulling the team along.

In 2011 and again in 2015, BGHS was recognized as an "A+ School of Excellence" by the Arizona Educational Foundation following an intense analysis by a team of people who scoured the school classrooms for three days. The award is for a three-year term, after which schools must reapply. The Center for the Future of Arizona declared BGHS a "Beat the Odds" school recently, too.

Andersen carries the same message of focus and relentless effort to his students, reminding them almost every day that complacency has no place at Barry Goldwater High School. During one morning's announcements, he used the PA to "celebrate the extraordinary efforts" over the weekend—a "huge" football victory and a large marching band festival hosted by BGHS and attended by 27 other bands from around the state.

"[These students] are demonstrating what quality is all about here," Andersen told the student body. "So make sure you are focused on quality work. There's enough mediocrity in the world; we certainly don't need to add any more to it."

"Have a wonderful day," he signed off, and then added, "Do all the little things that matter."

CHAPTER 3

Managing Change

Cherrelyn Elementary in Englewood, Colorado, serves a predominantly low-income neighborhood in the south metro Denver area. Seventy-five percent of the students are eligible for free or reduced-price lunch, 15 percent are English language learners, and roughly 15 percent are classified as homeless. The challenges of the low-performing school were obvious to Eva Pasiewicz when she became principal—and she knew exactly what to do.

Pasiewicz, who grew up in a similar neighborhood in Chicago, says she came into the job "like a bull in a china shop." At first, she says, "I was just bulldozing over the teachers and saying, 'This is how we're going to do things; let's go do it.'"

It was the same approach that had burned her out at her first principal job in Rifle, Colorado, just a few years earlier. For Pasiewicz, a former physical education teacher and wilderness survival expert, taking charge and getting things done is instinctual. But as she discovered in Rifle, such single-minded determination may earn you praise from your superintendent but not necessarily from your staff. After two years of working harder than she ever had, she found her teachers were unhappy, she didn't have much support, and she wondered if she was doing the job the way she was supposed to.

"I had an administrator's certificate, but I didn't know how to lead a group of teachers," she says.

Pasiewicz quit and stayed away from education for a while, trying a different career path and doing a lot of traveling. Eventually she wanted to return to education and found herself back in Colorado, applying for a principal position in Englewood.

Change is hard, Pasiewicz has learned. Sometimes you encounter resistance. Often, it's distractions. As she notes, there's always something going on in the school that redirects the day and takes energy away from managing teachers. On a recent morning, Pasiewicz received notice that a student's father had passed away suddenly, dealt with the consequences of the absence (day four) of a teacher whose son's illness remained undiagnosed, and attended an unscheduled meeting at the district office. "You think your day is going to go one way, and then *boom,*" she snaps her fingers, "something happens and it goes a whole other way. Often I never get anything done."

Pasiewicz's plight is hardly unique and may account for the high burnout and turnover rate among school leaders. State and district studies have found that turnover rates for principals range from 20 percent in Milwaukee and North Carolina, to 22 percent in Miami-Dade, 24 percent in New York City, 26 percent in San Francisco, and 30 percent in Texas (Béteille, Kalogrides, & Loeb, 2011). The cumulative effective of this turnover means that an average principal stays in his or her current school for only a few years. A Texas study, for example concluded that the "average high school principal will not see his/her first freshman class graduate" (Fuller, 2012, n.p.). More troubling, principals are probably not sticking around long enough to see results of their improvement initiatives, which can often take several years to bear fruit (Seashore-Louis, Leithwood, Wahlstrom, & Anderson, 2010).

A key factor behind this turnover rate appears to be principals' struggles to effect change in their schools. Often, it seems, the harder they push for results, the harder teachers push back. Interviews with 12 principals who quit the profession, for example, found that 9 left because they were dissatisfied with the job (Johnson, 2005). Most took the position wanting "to influence and help children" or "work with teachers" as instructional leaders, but they found that bureaucratic roadblocks, overwhelming workloads, and struggles to persuade teachers to adopt new initiatives made the job frustrating and unrewarding (Johnson, 2005, p. 22).

Echoing these findings, a more recent series of case studies of principals found that a key to principal stability appeared to be the ability to create "collaboration and cohesiveness" among school teachers (Burkhauser, Gates, Hamilton, & Ikemoto, 2012, p. xv), something almost half of principals struggled to do. The experiences of principals reflect the current reality that school leaders often have great responsibility, shouldering much of the burden of accountability systems, with little authority to select staff, allocate resources, or make programmatic decisions (Finn, 2012). They lead something that school and organizational researcher Karl Weick (1982) long ago labeled a "loosely coupled" system, in which they have, at best, loose control over teachers.

As a result, effective school leadership is less about giving orders and more about leading through social persuasion, personal connections, and shared leadership. It is perhaps not surprising, then, that among the key takeaways researchers drew from their case studies is the notion that the most successful new principals spent time meeting one-on-one with every teacher and eliciting from them ideas for improving student achievement, rather than imposing top-down directives (Burkhauser et al., 2012).

The good news is that becoming more effective at managing change appears to be a learned behavior. Indeed, a recent scientific study of the Balanced Leadership program (Jacob, Goddard, Kim, Miller, & Goddard, 2014) found that principals in the program significantly increased their awareness of key leadership behaviors associated with guiding and managing change—and, perhaps most important, were far less likely than nonparticipants to leave their positions. One reason for their willingness to stay put and see their efforts through may well be increased understanding and ability to act upon four big ideas about change.

Four Big Ideas About Change

All three components of the Balanced Leadership Framework are critical, but for most leaders, managing change is where the rubber meets the road—and the wheels are likely to come off. If your staff doesn't support the changes that your school needs to make, and if you can't manage the change process effectively from start to finish, the best focus and greatest plan in the world won't matter. Your efforts will stall or fail.

Schools change often, but most changes are surface changes. Real change requires leading people into the unknown, where they have to confront and change their own values and beliefs about teaching and learning.

When leading difficult changes, leaders must serve as catalysts for change, shaking up the status quo and articulating a new vision for the school. That said, they can't simply, as in Eva Pasiewicz's case, plow through it like a bull in a china shop. They must also be attentive to and aware of what is going on around them—namely, that change is never easy for people. They must keep the lines of communication open, listen to what people are going through, help them reexamine attitudes and beliefs, and ensure they have the training or resources needed to do what's expected.

Most likely you have been part of several change initiatives—both successful and not—either as the leader responsible for managing the change or as part of the community being asked to make changes. Through your experiences, you may have developed your own theory of action about how the change process works. Based on those experiences, how would you answer the following two questions?

- What motivates people to change?
- Why do some changes last and others do not?

For decades, these questions have been the focus of opinion, theory building, and research (i.e., Waters & Cameron, 2007), and there are many helpful resources available to leaders who try to answer them. Over the years, researchers at McREL have arrived at four conclusions about change for school leaders to consider as they embark on their own change initiatives: (1) change lies in the eye of the beholder, (2) misreading change can have an adverse effect on student achievement, (3) leaders need to adjust their approach based on the change at hand, and (4) change is a complex and iterative process.

Big Idea: Change Lies in the Eye of the Beholder

How would you feel if someone asked you to sing in front of a large group? Skydive? Move to another state? Your comfort level with each activity may differ and may be very different from your colleague's comfort level with the same activity. Maybe you'd love to try sky diving, but the thought of moving makes you panic. In your mind, these two activities represent two different kinds of change. If you view a change as a relatively straightforward step, it is likely first-order change. If you perceive a change as a disruptive experience, you perceive that change as second order. The way you perceive the action being asked of you undoubtedly affects how you proceed.

Consider for a moment a difficult change you've made—maybe it was tossing out a traditional grading system in favor of standards-based competencies, creating multiage classrooms, or engaging in team teaching. Perhaps some of these changes were easy for you—or at least compelling enough to feel exciting. Conversely, you may have experienced personal anguish over what others seemed to see as a straightforward solution. Perhaps a new curriculum forced you to discard a favorite teaching unit, or changing enrollment patterns required that you to teach a new subject or grade level, or budget cuts eliminated the assistant principal position.

Heifetz and Laurie (1997) drew a similar distinction between what they labeled as "technical problems," which can be solved with existing knowledge and solutions, and "adaptive challenges," which require solutions that lie far outside our current modes of operation. For some, solving a technical problem may cause immense angst. Others may find an adaptive challenge exhilarating and professionally rewarding—something they've been waiting their whole careers to do. That's why it's important to consider both the overall school context of change (technical problem vs. adaptive challenge) and its personal implications for the stakeholders—whether they are likely to view the change as a relatively straightforward next step (first-order change), or as a discomfiting, personally and professionally challenging break from the past (second-order change). It's important to note that few changes can be labeled the same way for all stakeholders; rather, the same change will likely be viewed as first order for some and second order for others. See Figure 3.1 for a quick explanation about the two orders of change.

FIGURE 3.1

Characteristics of First-Order and Second-Order Change

FIRST-ORDER CHANGE IS CHANGE THAT IS PERCEIVED AS . . .	SECOND-ORDER CHANGE IS CHANGE THAT IS PERCEIVED AS . . .
• An extension of the past	• A break with the past
• Within the existing paradigm	• Outside the existing paradigm or modes of operation
• Consistent with prevailing values and norms	• Conflicting with prevailing norms and values
• Implemented with existing knowledge and skills	• Requires new knowledge and skills

Big Idea: Misreading Change Can Adversely Affect Student Achievement

So why is any of this important? As noted earlier, one of the more puzzling aspects of our early meta-analysis on school leadership was the presence of principals who had received high marks on many measures from their teachers, yet the performance of their schools remained low. One explanation was that these principals might have had the wrong focus for their leadership efforts. Another is that they might have been focusing their leadership initiatives on the right school and classroom practices, yet employing the wrong leadership behaviors for the *kind of change* they were leading. For example, they may have been using strategies that work well with changes perceived as first order, but are less effective with changes perceived as second order (or vice versa). In other words, without determining the magnitude of the change correctly, leaders might be slowing down their initiatives by turning a technical problem into a adaptive challenge; conversely, they may be bulldozing their way into an adaptive challenge with too much directivity and become mired in conflict or resistance. See Leadership Tool #6 for help in determining the magnitude of change that you must address for your stakeholders to adapt to your initiative.

Big Idea: Leaders Need to Adjust Their Approach Based on the Change at Hand

Years ago, our colleagues were mired in debate about school improvement. One team of experts argued that low-performing schools needed clear

Estimating the Magnitude of a Change

Purpose: This tool is designed to help school leaders estimate the magnitude of a change from the perspective of individuals and stakeholder groups.

Directions:

1. Review the bundle of key improvement activities identified in Leadership Tool #4.

2. Use the questions in this tool to determine if your changes are likely to be perceived as first order or second order.

3. Select a stakeholder group (e.g., teachers, parents, or students) and answer each question based on what you think that group's perceptions might be. Determine if the change has first-order or second-order implications.

STAKEHOLDER GROUP: _____

Is new knowledge required for your change initiative? If so, what?	In what ways does the change initiative build on, or overturn, past practices?	In what ways is the change initiative congruent or incongruent with stakeholders' personal beliefs?	In what ways is the change initiative congruent or incongruent with prevailing organizational norms?
Would the majority of stakeholders perceive the new knowledge required by the change initiative to be easily learned using existing knowledge and skills?	Would the majority of stakeholders perceive the change initiative as an extension of the past?	Would the majority of the stakeholders perceive the change initiative as congruent with their personal values and beliefs?	Would the majority of the stakeholders perceive the change initiative as consistent with the prevailing norms?
☐ YES ☐ NO	☐ YES ☐ NO	☐ YES ☐ NO	☐ YES ☐ NO

If you answered "no" to any of the questions, your change initiative is likely an adaptive challenge with *second-order implications* for the selected stakeholders.

direction, perhaps some sort of unambiguous playbook for raising student achievement. This playbook typically consisted of getting teachers to adopt a few simple but crucial teaching routines (such as direct vocabulary instruction) that could quickly boost achievement. In short, leaders needed to push change from the top down and use a directive approach.

Another team insisted that dysfunctional cultures were usually at the heart of poor school performance; thus, schools needed to craft a common vision for success and develop shared agreements for working together to support students. In other words, leaders need to encourage change and empower stakeholders to have a voice in change. Yes, it took longer, but ultimately it led to more sustained improvement.

Both teams had evidence to support their approaches. Schools working with the first team had demonstrated rapid achievement gains. Schools working with the second team had shown equally dramatic, albeit less immediate, gains.

So which approach works best?

As it turns out, this same debate is reflected in literature and research on leadership. On one hand, some advocate for (and some studies point to) the value of a more *directive* style of leadership. In fact, in many environments and situations, directiveness and efficiency appears to go hand in hand, especially when higher performance is tied to better execution of routine tasks. A study of health care teams in Israel, for example, found that teams whose leaders were empowering or participatory demonstrated greater reflection and innovation, yet lower overall performance—presumably because "team reflection may be important for more complex tasks, such as innovative acts, but redundant for routine tasks" (Somech, 2006, p. 151).

Directive leadership behaviors may get quick results, but over the long haul, such behaviors may have diminishing returns on performance. What may be needed instead is a more *empowering* leadership style. Consider a study involving 60 teams of college seniors engaged in a multiperson, military-style computer simulation. It found that teams led by directive leaders—those who assigned individuals to roles, gave clear directions, and set expectations for compliance—initially outperformed other teams. Those other teams were led by empowering leaders—those who shared power, encouraged dissenting opinions, and promoted shared decision making. Over the course of repeated trials, though, the performance of teams with directive leaders began to plateau. Meanwhile, teams led by empowering leaders continued to improve and eventually eclipsed those with directive leaders. The researchers concluded that empowering leadership made teams initially less productive as they sorted out how they would work together, but ultimately this process supported greater collaborative learning and continued improvement in performance (Lorinkova, Pearsall, & Sims, 2013).

A similar argument can be made in school settings: To get quick gains in achievement, reflection and innovation may be less important than simply executing teaching routines more effectively and implementing the curriculum more consistently.

Profiles of two dozen beat-the-odds (high-poverty and high-performing) schools conducted by Karin Chenoweth (2007, 2009) demonstrate this pattern. Many of these schools, especially at the elementary level, established new instructional routines through what one might call prepackaged curricula like America's Choice, Success for All, Everyday Math, Open Court, and Core Knowledge. School leaders made it clear that every teacher was expected to deliver the new curriculum. Thus the schools did away with what one beat-the-odds school leader in Philadelphia described as the "Burger King" model, in which teachers "got to have it their way" (Chenoweth, 2007, p. 128). Making these changes resulted in immediate and dramatic improvements in performance.

Within a few years, many of the schools with prepackaged curriculum began to adapt their curriculum, working together to better align it with their students' needs. Earlier research (Goodwin, 2011b) found a similar pattern of empowerment among high-performing, high-poverty schools. Teachers in these schools were more likely than teachers in low-performing schools to report having influence in school decisions and a shared vision for success. Simply stated, they had learned how to come together to develop new approaches and ways of working together to get things done.

As schools improve, though, they're likely to reach a performance ceiling where the way forward becomes ambiguous. A school that has experienced gains by enacting a curriculum and ensuring greater consistency in student learning experiences may find itself facing a thornier challenge—perhaps figuring out how to motivate students to engage in and buy into their own learning. Here, the way forward is not clear. It likely lies in teams of teachers coming together to identify new ways of igniting students' passion for learning, perhaps by unleashing their creativity and passions through immersive project-based learning opportunities. As you may have already guessed, leading these two types of change requires very different leadership styles, as shown in Figure 3.2, p. 44.

We might think of these different leadership styles as being able to understand when a leader needs to step up and direct the implementation of a technical solution versus when he or she needs to step back and hand some decision making to others, allowing stakeholders to learn together and develop new solutions. As we mentioned in the Introduction, knowing when and how to balance one's leadership style is crucial to effective leadership (and the reason we call the entire concept *Balanced Leadership*).

FIGURE 3.2

Leadership Styles and Types of Change

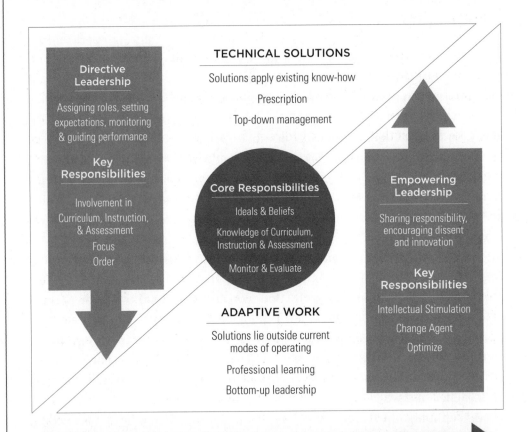

We detected the same pattern in a follow-up study to our original meta-analysis on school leadership. As you'll recall from our discussion in Chapter 1, the follow-up study began with our survey of 659 principals, asking them to describe the complexity of the change initiative in which they were engaged and which leadership behaviors they felt they were fulfilling well and which they were struggling to do well. The subsequent factor analysis detected a positive association between principals reporting that they were in the midst of addressing *first-order* change and all 21 leadership responsibilities. In short, every leadership responsibility seemed to come into play. That said, the study found that some leadership responsibilities were more tightly linked with guiding first-order or technical solutions than others. Here are the top seven, in rank order:

1. Monitor and Evaluate
2. Culture
3. Ideals and Beliefs

4. Knowledge of Curriculum, Instruction, and Assessment

5. Involvement in Curriculum, Instruction, and Assessment

6. Focus

7. Order

However, as noted in Chapter 1, when it comes to guiding *second-order* changes, we found *positive* associations with 7 of the 21 responsibilities (shown in Figure 3.3) and *negative* associations with 4 responsibilities (shown in Figure 3.4).

When we consider these results a bit more, they are not altogether surprising. They suggest that a top-down, directive leadership style may be best suited to ensuring proper implementation of a straightforward or first-order solution, which require leaders to closely manage the effort through *Involvement in Curriculum, Instruction, and Assessment*, while maintaining *Focus* and *Order*. However, as challenges become less technical and more adaptive or second order, leaders may need to pivot to a different set of behaviors, which include challenging the status quo (serving as a *Change Agent*), inspiring people to innovate and take on challenges that may seem initially beyond their reach (*Optimize*), and encouraging shared learning about current best practices and research (*Intellectual Stimulation*).

The fact that *Culture*, *Communication*, *Order*, and *Input* all appear to suffer during adaptive challenges is not surprising, either. Adaptive challenges by their very nature bring a great deal of ambiguity to the scene and often require new ways of working together and a new mindset—one that eschews following ready-made scripts or procedures in favor of experimentation and learning from mistakes. All this can cause feelings of disorientation, breakdowns in communication, and feelings of personal vulnerability. Meanwhile, the uncertainty can increase participants' needs for processing, input, and dialogue; make leaders seem less accessible; and stakeholders' voices less influential in the decision-making process. Regardless of how much additional attention and effort a principal may give to these responsibilities, teachers and other stakeholders may perceive that their leaders are not fulfilling them.

Maintaining consistency with core leadership responsibilities

It's worth noting that regardless of whether the changes are perceived as first or second order, a few core leadership responsibilities appear to remain constant, including consistently communicating the moral purpose of the changes (*Ideals and Beliefs*), demonstrating expertise in the core business of the school (*Knowledge of Curriculum, Instruction, and Assessment*), and remaining closely involved in the changes themselves (*Monitor and Evaluate*). In other words, even when leading technical problems, leaders still need to tie the effort back to a deeper, moral purpose (starting with "why"). They cannot simply adopt a do-it-because-I-said-so approach. At the same time,

Figure 3.3

Responsibilities Positively Correlated with Second-Order Change (in Rank Order)

LEADERSHIP RESPONSIBILITIES	THE EXTENT TO WHICH THE PRINCIPAL . . .	PRACTICES USED TO FULFILL RESPONSIBILITIES
Knowledge of Curriculum, Instruction, and Assessment	Is knowledgeable about current curriculum, instruction, and assessment practices	• Possesses extensive knowledge about effective curricular, instructional, and assessment activities • Provides conceptual guidance regarding effective classroom practices
Optimize	Inspires and leads new and challenging innovations	• Inspires teachers to accomplish things that might be beyond their grasp • Is the driving force behind major initiatives • Portrays a positive attitude about the ability of the staff to accomplish substantial things
Intellectual Stimulation	Ensures faculty and staff are aware of the most current theories and practices, and makes the discussion of these a regular aspect of the school's culture	• Keeps informed about current research and theory on effective schooling • Continually exposes the staff to cutting-edge research and theory on effective schooling • Fosters systematic discussion regarding current research and theory on effective schooling
Change Agent	Is willing to challenge and actively challenge the status quo	• Consciously challenges the status quo • Is willing to lead change initiatives with uncertain outcomes • Systematically considers new and better ways of doing things • Consistently attempts to operate at the edge versus the center of the school's competence
Monitor and Evaluate	Monitors the effectiveness of school practices and their impact on student learning	• Continually monitors the effectiveness of the school's curricular, instruction, and assessment practices • Remains aware of the impact of the school's practices on student achievement
Flexibility	Adapts his or her leadership behavior to the needs of the current situation and is comfortable with dissent	• Is comfortable with making major changes in how things are done • Encourages people to express diverse opinions contrary to those held by individuals in positions of authority • Adapts leadership style to the needs of specific situations • Is directive or nondirective as the situation warrants
Ideals and Beliefs	Communicates and operates from strong ideals and beliefs about schooling	• Possesses well-defined beliefs about schools, teaching, and learning • Shares beliefs about schools, teaching, and learning with the staff • Demonstrates behaviors that are consistent with beliefs

FIGURE 3.4

Responsibilities Negatively Correlated with Second-Order Change (in Rank Order)

LEADERSHIP RESPONSIBILITIES	THE EXTENT TO WHICH THE PRINCIPAL . . .	PRACTICES USED TO FULFILL RESPONSIBILITIES
Culture	Fosters shared beliefs and a sense of community and cooperation	• Promotes a sense of well-being among teachers and staff • Promotes cohesion among teachers and staff • Develops an understanding of purpose among teachers and staff • Develops a shared vision of what the school could be like • Promotes cooperation among teachers and staff
Communication	Establishes strong lines of communication with and among teachers and students	• Is easily accessible to teachers and staff • Develops effective means for teachers and staff to communicate with one another • Maintains open and effective lines of communication with teachers and staff
Order	Establishes a set of standard operating procedures and routines	• Provides and reinforces clear structures, rules, and procedures for teachers and staff • Provides and reinforces clear structures, rules, and procedures for students • Establishes routines for the effective running of the school that teachers and staff understand and follow
Input	Involves teachers in the design and implementation of important decisions and policies	• Provides opportunities for teacher and staff input on all important decisions • Provides opportunities for teachers and staff to be involved in developing school policies • Uses leadership teams in decision making

empowering people to tackle adaptive challenges does not mean that leaders should be hands-off with the effort; to the contrary, they must closely monitor and evaluate what's happening.

At this point, a caveat is in order. Scientific study of the change process might leave the impression that it can all be managed with neat if/then decision trees that tell leaders exactly what to do at each step. In reality, though, as with anything that involves people, change is messy. Even the simplest, most straightforward change can become immensely complicated. That's because every change requires people to break old habits, engage in new behaviors, and feel (initially, at least) incompetent. Change is always personal.

Big Idea: Change Is a Complex and Iterative Process

Effective change leadership requires a deep understanding of the change process, which is complex, nonlinear, and recursive (see Figure 3.5). To assist leaders in understanding this process, we define it through four phases: (1) Create Demand, (2) Implement, (3) Monitor and Evaluate, and (4) Manage Personal Transitions. It's critical for school leaders to understand how the phases of change work together.

First, the phases are highly *interdependent*. For example, successful implementation requires effective management of personal transitions, which is based on closely monitoring the implementation of a change. Monitoring and evaluating the quality, fidelity, consistency, and intensity of implementation may increase or decrease demand for change.

Second, the phases of change are not sequential; they are *recursive*. For example, at the implementation phase, leaders may continue to create demand as a means to revitalize change initiatives that are losing ground.

Third, the change process is substantially *different for change perceived as first-order compared with change perceived as second order*. When a school experiences a change with first-order implications for its stakeholders, the change process generally cycles through these three phases: create demand, implement, and monitor and evaluate. However, if a change has second-order implications for stakeholders, the process has an additional phase that we call manage personal transitions. Thus, the change process will be different depending on the magnitude of change perceived by the stakeholders. This difference means that school leaders must be highly attuned to their staff, organization, community, the magnitude of change implied by the improvement initiative, and the phases of change. Let's dig deeper into each of the phases of change.

FIGURE 3.5
Phases of Change

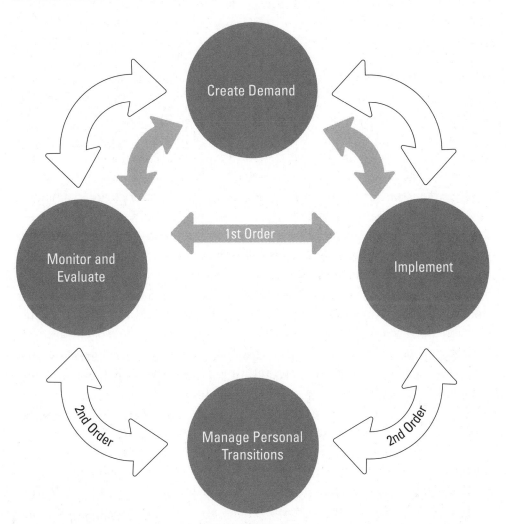

Source: Adapted from *The Balanced Leadership Framework: Connecting Vision with Action* (p. 33), by J. T. Waters & G. Cameron, 2007, Aurora, CO: McREL. Copyright © 2007 by McREL.

Phase 1: Create Demand

Little change occurs in a school that accepts or is satisfied with the status quo. Thus, leadership serves as the catalyst for creating demand—or disequilibrium. Indeed, the driving force behind any major change is the recognition that the status quo is no longer sustainable and that a better alternative exists. Knowing this, school leaders must *actively challenge the status quo* by simultaneously creating discontent with the current reality *and* developing a vision of a more attractive future state.

In *Bounce: The Art of Turning Tough Times into Triumph*, business writer Keith McFarland (2009) describes two types of anxiety: anxiety about change and anxiety about what will happen if we *don't* change. Too much anxiety about change hurts performance. In fact, a great deal of research shows that when people are in a state of fear, they are more likely to make mistakes and less likely to innovate (Bronson & Merryman, 2013). Great leaders, writes McFarland, absorb the first kind of often very personal anxiety (e.g., Will I lose my job?) and redirect it into a second kind of more productive, cooperative anxiety (e.g., What must we do together so no one loses his or her job?).

The most effective school leaders use both of these techniques. Often they start with data to point out that the status quo is not sustainable—that the current downward (or flat) trend is untenable. In short, they make the current reality so unpleasant that people are willing to accept the risk and discomfort associated with changing it. Good leaders, of course, don't stop there.

They also develop a vision of a more attractive reality and help everyone envision that new, brighter future (e.g., "Imagine our students coming to school happy or returning years from now to tell us all how successful they are in life"). If the vision is compelling enough (for adaptive challenges) or the next steps clear and concrete enough (for technical problems), people become more willing to engage in change, despite whatever risk and discomfort may be associated with it. When the tension between the current reality and the anticipation of a preferred future is great enough, it motivates individuals or groups to move beyond the status quo.

Sometimes mere discomfort isn't enough to compel people to change—or stick with a change effort. As Alan Deutschman (2006) notes in *Change or Die*, when cardiac-bypass patients are told by their surgeons that they must change their lifestyle (perhaps by changing their diet, exercising more, quitting smoking, reducing alcohol intake, and curbing stress) or they will wind up back on the operating table—or worse, six feet under—only 1 in 10 are actually able to do so. In school settings, we might reasonably ask, if fear of death isn't enough to get people to change behavior, what makes us think that the mere fear of losing their jobs will?

Deutschman concluded from examples like this one and other research studies that the three *F*s of "fear, facts, and force" are usually insufficient to drive sustained changes in behavior—whether it's a health change or changes in a company or an organization. What's more effective are the three *R*s of "relate, repeat, and reframe." In short, people are more likely to change when they can *relate* to the person asking them to change (or others engaged in the same process), have opportunities to *repeat* the change while being supported by others, and finally, have the challenge *reframed* for them in a way that inspires new thinking and new hope. For example, instead of focusing on the things they're giving up (e.g., smoking, drinking, eating favorite foods), the focus is on what they're gaining (e.g., greater energy, better physique, higher self-esteem, and a longer life).

The research suggests that when motivating change, the traditional notions of *extrinsic* rewards—commonly referred to as "carrots and sticks"—are often less effective than focusing on key drivers of *intrinsic* motivation. In *Drive: The Surprising Truth About What Motivates Us*, Daniel Pink (2009) synthesizes decades of research on intrinsic motivation into three key drivers of change: giving people some choice in or control over what they're being asked to do (*autonomy*), helping them to see themselves progressing toward their goal (*mastery*), and finding deeper meaning in what they're being asked to do (*purpose*). This third aspect of intrinsic motivation can be easy to overlook. But as Simon Sinek (2011) notes in his book (and accompanying TED Talk) *Start with Why*, "People don't buy what you do, they buy why you do it." For example, Martin Luther King Jr. inspired people of all races to support the civil rights movement not because of the *what* of the movement—for example, engaging in sit-ins to protest desegregated lunch counters—but because of the deeper moral purpose, or *why*—namely, that when society's laws conflict with higher law, we should follow the latter. The same could be said of school improvement efforts. What people are likely to find more compelling is not the *what* (e.g., implementing the Frayer model of vocabulary instruction in all classrooms) but the *why* (e.g., rapidly building students' background knowledge so they can all be successful).

As it turns out, our meta-analysis identified three key leadership responsibilities that reflect these principles at the heart of effective school leadership (see Figure 3.6). First, great leaders operate as a *Change Agent*, often using data to challenge the status quo and providing a vision for a better future. In addition, they use research and best practices to challenge people's thinking about what's possible and help them reframe their expectations, something we identified as *Intellectual Stimulation*. Finally, great leaders consistently articulate the moral purpose, or the why, behind the initiative, helping everyone in the school understand that they are there to serve students and provide them with better life outcomes, a responsibility we identified in our research as *Ideals and Beliefs*. Tool #7 (p. 54) provides a guide for specifying how you might approach each of these responsibilities.

Phase 2: Implement

All too often, change initiatives fail because leaders assume that the demand created in the first phase will carry the initiative forward. Sustaining the sense of urgency and vision created in Phase 1 requires developing a deep and shared understanding of the concrete actions the change requires while keeping sight of the intended outcome. Our research indicates that two of the seven leadership responsibilities positively associated with second-order change are especially helpful during this implementation phase: *Knowledge of Curriculum, Instruction, and Assessment* and *Optimize* (see Figure 3.7, p. 53).

FIGURE 3.6

Leadership Responsibilities Associated with Phase 1: Create Demand

RESPONSIBILITIES	CLASSROOM AND SCHOOL PRACTICES
Change Agent: *Is willing to challenge and actively challenges the status quo*	• Consciously challenges the status quo • Is willing to lead change initiatives with uncertain outcomes • Systematically considers new and better ways of doing things • Consistently attempts to operate at the edge versus the center of the school's competence
Intellectual Stimulation: *Ensures faculty and staff are aware of the most current theories and practices and makes the discussion of these a regular aspect of the school culture*	• Keeps informed about current research and theory on effective schooling • Continually exposes teachers and staff to cutting-edge research and theory on effective schooling • Fosters systematic discussion regarding current research and theory on effective schooling
Ideals and Beliefs: *Communicates and operates from strong ideals and beliefs about schooling*	• Possesses well-defined beliefs about school, teaching, and learning • Shares beliefs about school, teaching, and learning with the teachers and staff • Demonstrates behaviors that are consistent with beliefs

Get involved

Principals must be highly knowledgeable about curriculum, instruction, and assessment as well as the research-based practices associated with the change initiative (the *why*) to provide ongoing conceptual guidance on the effort. Doing so typically requires in-depth reading about research-based practices, observing the desired change in other schools and districts, and participating alongside teachers in professional development opportunities.

Frame the message to create broad ownership

As discussed in greater detail in Tool #8 (see p. 56), it's important that people remain focused on the initiative when the going gets tough, and this requires framing (or reframing) change initiatives in such a way that people take ownership of implementing the effort and are intrinsically motivated to see it through. One of the key practices associated with the leadership responsibility of *Optimize* involves framing change initiatives to highlight the relative advantages of the effort and providing exemplars of a preferred future that can be emulated—that is, concrete examples of where you are heading.

FIGURE 3.7

Leadership Responsibilities Associated with Phase 2: Implement

RESPONSIBILITIES	CLASSROOM AND SCHOOL PRACTICES
Knowledge of Curriculum, Instruction, and Assessment: Is knowledgeable about current curriculum, instruction, and assessment practices	• Possesses extensive knowledge about effective curricular, instructional, and assessment practices • Provides conceptual guidance regarding effective classroom practices
Optimize: Inspires and leads new and challenging innovations	• Inspires teachers and staff to accomplish things that might be beyond their grasp • Is the driving force behind major initiatives • Portrays a positive attitude about the ability of teachers and staff to accomplish substantial things

Stay on message

You may recall that one of the three *R*s from *Change or Die* (Deutschman, 2006) is *repeat*. Getting change efforts to stick and to overcome a "this too shall pass" mentality often requires clear, consistent, ongoing communication. Leaders need to stay on message and make it clear that the change initiative is not going to disappear and insist that it remain a front-and-center focus for everyone.

Accentuate the positive

As you embark on any new initiative, you can be almost certain that your organization will encounter some disappointments. Every great organization faces setbacks on its road to success. In fact, Keith McFarland (2009) notes that great organizations tend to be forged in the fires of trying times. The key to staying on course with implementation of any effort, then, is helping people in the organization to develop what psychologist Martin Seligman (1990) describes as "learned optimism."

To illustrate, imagine two basketball players who both miss game-winning shots. A player with learned optimism is likely to respond by thinking, "That's not like me," and begin working to figure out what he or she did wrong and could do differently next time to go home a hero. A player with learned helplessness, on the other hand, is likely to conclude, "I'm no good at this game," and may even chalk up a clutch basket to pure luck. Seligman notes, however, that such attitudes are *learned*, or acquired, through experience.

Because they're learned, they can also be *unlearned* through "mastery experiences," which are opportunities to experience success, even on a small scale. The cumulative effect of small successes, according to Seligman, is that

Creating Demand

Purpose: This tool is designed to help school leaders plan for the Create Demand phase of the change process.

Directions:

1. Recall the improvement bundle identified in your Leadership Tool #4.

2. Determine how you plan to create discontent with the current reality (i.e., how you will reframe people's anxieties about change into a vision of a more attractive reality).

3. Determine how you will link your improvement initiative to a deeper "why," or moral purpose.

4. Identify the specific actions you will take to emphasize the responsibilities of *Change Agent, Intellectual Stimulation,* and *Ideals and Beliefs.*

5. Identify the evidence you will collect to show these actions were taken and their impact.

Change Agent—What techniques will you use to create discontent with current reality?

Actions:

Evidence:

Intellectual Stimulation—How will you reframe people's thinking to envision a more attractive reality?

Actions:

Evidence:

Ideals and Beliefs—How will you communicate the moral purpose, or deeper "why," for your initiative?

Actions:

Evidence:

they begin to show people that their successes are not the result of chance, but of their own efforts and competence. Great leaders develop a sense of learned optimism by helping people interpret disappointments as temporary and isolated, and successes as permanent and pervasive.

Identify opinion leaders and get them on board

When you are leading the change process and proceeding from creating demand to implementation, you will want to think strategically about opinion leaders on your staff. In his groundbreaking book, *Diffusion of Innovations*, Everett Rogers defines opinion leadership as "the degree to which an individual is able to influence other individuals' attitudes or overt behavior informally in a desired way with relative frequency" (2003, p. 27).

When opinion leaders support an improvement initiative, they can influence and encourage other staff members to adopt new research-based practices. It's likely that many of your school's opinion leaders are members of the leadership team. But many others may be spread across your school. Here are some questions that you can use to help you identify opinion leaders:

- Who in our school or community influences others' thinking?
- Who enjoys being recognized as having influence?
- Who knows a lot of people in the school and community?
- Who is viewed by others as knowledgeable and sincere?
- Who is willing to take risks by letting his or her opinions be known?

As you identify the opinion leaders in your school or district, you'll want to use Tool #8 to identify how you can strategically frame your improvement initiatives to make it more likely that these opinion leaders will not only buy in, but also take ownership of the effort and persuade others to follow.

Great leaders learn to target communication and highlight aspects of the change initiative that are most relevant to specific audiences. To do that, you must know the individuals in your organization well enough to select messages that will resonate with them, that will connect with those things that give them a sense of moral purpose, and that inspire them to go above and beyond the call of duty. In school settings, strong vision statements often connect to the reasons people entered the field of education.

As noted earlier, one key to motivating people to change their behavior is *reframing* a challenge in a way that helps them to think differently about an idea or concept, offering new hope or perspective on the challenge. Skillful framing helps people align change initiatives with their own personal beliefs and values. You want to frame your initiatives so that all stakeholders, especially opinion leaders, see the advantage of implementing the change and want to sustain the momentum.

Framing an Initiative to Become a Shared Vision

Purpose: This tool is designed to assist with the intentional thought and planning that are necessary to effectively frame initiatives so that they become a shared vision. In this case, it will help you to consider how you might employ one (or more) of five common framing devices used in public oratory (Gamson & Lasch, 1982) to help people embrace a change initiative: metaphors, catch phrases, exemplars, depictions, and visual images.

Directions:

1. Review Table 1, which gives descriptions and examples of the five framing devices.

2. Review Table 2, where you identify a Target Initiative (in this case, Implementing a Standards-Based Grading System), identify the stakeholders, choose the messages that will resonate with them (i.e., why the initiative matters to them), and select the framing devices that are likely to encourage long-term ownership of the initiative.

3. Complete Table 3 using your own Target Initiative. Although the example in Table 2 includes three stakeholder groups, include as many as are necessary.

Table 1. Choosing a Framing Device

Framing device	Description	Example
Metaphors	Figures of speech and stories that invite comparison	A "Gore Tex" culture where teams "brave the elements" to solve problems
Catch phrase	A brief slogan that captures your intended outcome	"2 in 1" (2 years of student learning for every 1 year in school)
Exemplars	A model or vicarious experience to emulate	"Become the XX (a successful school) of our district"
Depictions	A memorable string of modifiers to capture your desired outcome	"Students who are literate, numerate, and curious"
Visual images	A captivating picture that helps people see what's possible	A photo of a previously struggling student reading aloud to classmates

Table 2. Target Initiative: Implementing a Standards-Based Grading System

Stakeholder Group	Why It Matters to Them	Framing Device
Students	Our students want to know what they will be expected to learn and have a way to monitor their own progress.	*Depiction*: Provide grade-level-appropriate stories of how well-known individuals from a variety of settings (athletes, entertainers, leaders, historical figures, scientists) set a goal, practiced, studied, monitored progress, and eventually met their goal.
Teachers	Our teachers want a system that monitors student growth objectively and reinforces excellence in achievement.	*Exemplar*: Provide an example of how standards-based lessons are scored and translated into a standards-based report card.
Parents	Our parents want an easy-to-understand report that show what their students know and can do as benchmarked to grade-level expectations.	*Visual Image*: Provide a detailed example of what the new report looks like with explanations of each section.

Table 3. Target Initiative: _____

Stakeholder Group	Why It Matters to Them	Framing Device
Students		
Teachers		
Parents		
Support staff		
Central office		
Community		

Implement with quality, fidelity, intensity, and consistency

With any improvement effort (personal or organizational), there's a tendency to revert to old habits or ways of doing things. According to research (Waters & Cameron, 2007), turning new routines or ways of working into new habits that effect real change requires a concerted focus on the implementation effort's quality, fidelity, intensity, and consistency (QFIC):

- *Quality* is the degree of skill, excellence, or effectiveness with which the effort is implemented.

- *Fidelity* is the extent to which new practices align with the core components or principles of the new method, approach, or program.

- *Intensity* is the frequency of conversations, energy, and resources focused on the new innovation or approach.

- *Consistency* is the extent to which the new approaches or practices are carried over time with established standards of quality, fidelity, and intensity.

The following scenario illustrates how a principal might focus on QFIC during the implementation phase.

Principal Smith and her staff were about to implement a new initiative. They had completed the preparatory stage, which included a comprehensive review of data, study groups reading and discussing research on effective practice, whole-staff and team-level meetings, and visits to several schools that had recently adopted initiatives. In addition, some staff members had attended a variety of professional development sessions and were having an ongoing conversation with the district's assistant superintendent for curriculum, instruction, and assessment. Together, they had selected a bundle of research-based instructional strategies to serve as the foundation for literacy education at their elementary school. Now it was time to begin the work of implementing the initiative.

Quality. The first order of business was to ensure that all teachers had what they needed to successfully implement the strategies in their classrooms, starting with in-depth professional development. In the spring, experts in using the selected strategies came to the school to lead the staff through a two-day class on effective practice. During this session, teachers were introduced to the new methodology, saw it modeled by the staff developers, and had opportunities to practice it and receive feedback from their colleagues. This session was followed by weekly team meetings in which grade-level teachers began planning for the implementation of the new approach in the upcoming year. Principal Smith and Assistant Principal Douglas attended the staff development sessions and team meetings. The conversations at these meetings focused on implementing a high-quality program. Assets were inventoried, resources were requested, and each team identified the supports they needed in order to be successful.

The school-level literacy team, made up of teachers from all grade levels, literacy specialists, and special-area teachers, also met weekly. They discussed the ideas being generated at the grade-level meetings, made final selection of and ordered the materials needed, began planning for ongoing staff development, and rescheduled the school day to allow for uninterrupted literacy blocks for every grade level.

Fidelity. Before the end of the year, the school's literacy team began working with teachers to construct a literacy framework that included the elements of the new initiative.

As the primary- and intermediate-grade-level teachers and specialists identified different elements, the team communicated to build consensus. At the last all-staff meeting of the year, the literacy team presented the complete framework. Because staff had been involved throughout the process, little fine-tuning was required. Staff agreed to use the framework to drive their literacy instruction during the coming year. They also agreed that the evaluation process for the coming year would revolve around literacy, and that the school administrator walk-throughs and ongoing peer observations and follow-up conversations would focus on literacy instruction using the framework. The administrators and the literacy team developed a shared understanding of what effective instruction, as defined in the framework, looked like in the classroom.

Intensity. The work to implement the new approach continued in the new school year. During the first week of school, Ms. Smith, Mr. Douglas, and teacher-coaches began visiting classrooms during the literacy blocks. Both students and teachers quickly became accustomed to having visitors in the classrooms. As the school year progressed and questions about instruction began to arise, staff meeting time was reserved for conversations about implementation. Weekly grade-level team meetings focused on sharing successes, challenges, and student work. Literacy team members embedded in each grade-level team addressed staff questions about professional development and resources.

The school's leadership team, made up of grade-level representatives, teacher-coaches, and school administrators, discussed the fact that this first year would result in a lot of learning—and unexpected challenges. This team communicated to the rest of the staff, through informal and formal channels, that they did not expect flawless implementation but did expect a relentless focus on getting better.

As the first trimester ended, data were collected and analyzed. Both grade-level and literacy teams looked at implementation and impact. Ongoing collection of formative data had been a part of the school's operational agreements before the new initiative, and it served them well. Ms. Smith and Mr. Douglas added to the conversation by reporting schoolwide patterns they had observed. Because classroom observations were confidential, the data were reported in generalities at the school level. No data on individual teachers or grade levels were shared.

Consistency. As the second trimester began, conversations turned to how to improve upon what they had already accomplished. Ms. Smith made a concerted effort to keep the grade-level literacy blocks free from interruptions. The literacy team enhanced the framework by setting expectations for how much literacy instruction would be guaranteed to each student in the school (e.g., each 3rd grader would participate in at least two guided reading groups with materials on his or her instructional level every week). In addition, the assistant superintendent for curriculum, instruction, and assessment directed teachers to discontinue some units that were not tied to district standards and to scale back nonacademic classroom practices, such as holiday parties. By the winter break, there was some discontent. Change that had originally been viewed as having first-order implications by some staff was now beginning to have second-order implications—the technical solution was beginning to feel a little more like an adaptive challenge, prompting Ms. Smith and her leadership team to consider innovative ways for helping teachers work together.

Ms. Smith's response to the rising discontent was to balance her leadership approach. It was time to stop directing and start empowering by setting up some ways in which teachers could step back and really look at what was happening around the school. She decided staff would spend the professional development day following the winter break looking at implementation and formative assessment data. The data affirmed that the teachers and students were making progress. Teachers also had expressed an interest in seeing how others were doing, as they had been talking about their changing classroom practice all year. In response, Ms. Smith and Mr. Douglas set up peer coaching triads and secured release time for each grade level to take turns doing peer observations. These observations were driven by the framework, and teachers engaged in post-observation conferences around the framework. In addition, she asked some teachers for permission to create videos of portions of their lessons. Ms. Smith and Mr. Douglas independently observed the video lessons through the lens of the framework and compared notes.

The literacy team also identified a lack of resources as the greatest barrier to the fidelity of the program. All grade levels had reported their need for a greater topical variety of text and for more books with specific reading-level bands. So they began a concerted effort to organize resources and add materials.

By year's end, displays of student work around the school and in school and district newsletters and websites communicated the school's successes. It was time for the leadership team to make plans for continuing the literacy focus next year. By pooling professional development monies, they would be able to hire the original literacy consultants for follow-up training during the summer. The literacy team selected books and articles that would extend and refine staff knowledge about literacy for the study groups that were offered before and after school. In addition, the assistant superintendent allocated funds for a small team of teachers to analyze perception, implementation, and achievement data over the summer. This group reported results to the superintendent and the school board.

With three teaching positions open for the coming year, the principal, assistant principal, and grade-level teams interviewed potential candidates and made hiring recommendations that included whether the candidates had proven experience teaching within a similar framework. They sought out candidates with a sincere desire to be part of the initiative's second year. Grade-level team members designed a literacy induction program to help the new teachers learn the school's literacy approach. During the next year, the new teachers were assigned to peer-coaching triads and had opportunities to observe classrooms and to watch and discuss model lessons with their mentors and school administration.

As this scenario suggests, the implementation phase is hard work. To truly get the results that are possible, a principal must continually *Optimize* and provide conceptual guidance around his or her *Knowledge of Curriculum, Instruction, and Assessment*. Tool #9 can help you clarify your thinking on these two responsibilities as they relate to implementation. Also, as we'll discuss in more detail in Phase 4 of the change process, a principal must demonstrate *Flexibility*, especially by being an active listener, encouraging, and responding to dissent.

Phase 3: Monitor and Evaluate

We know from the research of Bruce Joyce and Beverly Showers (2002) that introducing new concepts, modeling them, and providing opportunities for people to practice them are important but insufficient to create transfer of knowledge to actual practice. What drives transfer of knowledge is peer coaching—providing people with opportunities to help one another past inevitable sticking points in their professional growth. Old habits are hard to break and new ones even harder to develop. That's what Mary Budd Rowe, who first identified and popularized the concept of "wait time"—pausing for three seconds or longer after asking questions in order to elicit greater student participation—discovered in her follow-up research (1986). At first, when teachers pause after questions, the ensuing silence can seem unbearable; within a few days, they're able to feel more comfortable with the practice.

After three or four weeks of using longer wait times, however, teachers begin to revert back to old habits, and they needed support from peers and coaches to stick with the practice (Rowe, 1986). Thus, a key to proper implementation is providing ongoing feedback to staff on how they're doing with a

Implementation Plan

Purpose: This tool is designed to help school leaders plan for the Implementation phase of the change process.

Directions: Using the bundle of improvement efforts identified in Leadership Tool #4, determine how you plan to implement with quality, fidelity, intensity, and consistency.

1. Identify the specific actions you will take to emphasize the responsibilities of *Knowledge of Curriculum, Instruction, and Assessment* and *Optimize*.

2. Record the evidence you will collect to show these actions occurred and the impact they had.

What specifically do you need to know (*Knowledge of Curriculum, Instruction, and Assessment*) regarding this initiative that will provide credibility to your implementation plan?

Actions taken to attain knowledge:

Evidence of knowledge:

How will you inspire (*Optimize*) others by skillfully targeting and framing the initiative?

Actions taken to inspire others:

Evidence of inspiring others:

What are the relative advantages of this initiative?

How is this initiative compatible with your current practices?

What new skills and knowledge will staff require to implement this initiative?

---

new practice, which includes creating opportunities for people to learn from one another and to coach one another—and to prevent a backslide into the old ways.

We define Monitor and Evaluate as a specific phase of change; however, it really is an extension of the implementation process. As we saw in the QFIC scenario, it is through monitoring and evaluating that implementation becomes sustainable (see Figure 3.8). Decisions about how to proceed with the implementation of an initiative require the right data. Data help us make informed decisions about our policies, practices, and procedures in order to improve student achievement. Making data-based decisions is at the heart of continuous improvement.

FIGURE 3.8

Leadership Responsibility Associated with Phase 3: Monitor and Evaluate

RESPONSIBILITY	CLASSROOM AND SCHOOL PRACTICES
Monitor and Evaluate: *Monitors the effectiveness of school practices and their impact on student learning*	• Continually monitors the effectiveness of the school's curricular practices • Continually monitors the effectiveness of the school's instructional practices • Continually monitors the effectiveness of the school's assessment practices

Collecting and analyzing data on the quality, fidelity, intensity, and consistency of implementation requires school leaders to be skilled at the use of formative and summative data in evaluating the impact of an initiative on the desired outcomes. To accurately assess the effects of implementation on student achievement, school leaders must attend to leading indicators and skillfully use "holding environments" that let staff discuss and acknowledge concerns in a trusting environment. Tool #10 can help you plan how to proceed with this phase of the change process.

Phase 4: Manage Personal Transitions

School improvement initiatives often require stakeholders to undergo personal transitions, which they sometimes resist. Changes in programs and practices, which represent a *gain* for students, schools, or school districts, can be perceived as a *loss* for teachers or principals, especially when they must gain new knowledge, develop new approaches and procedures, redefine relationships, and reexamine their norms and values.

We think there is an important distinction between managing personal transitions created by second-order change and managing change itself. William Bridges (1991), author of *Managing Transitions: Making the Most of*

Change, makes the distinction between *change* and *transition* by describing the former as external and the latter as internal. *Personal transitions*, according to Bridges, are internal, personal, psychological processes that are often the result of *external changes*.

Managing personal transitions created by second-order change, understanding individual responses, and managing them effectively are imperative to successful change leadership.

Because personal transitions vary among individuals and among groups, principals must fulfill the leadership responsibility of *Flexibility*; that is, they must be flexible in their approach to leadership and differentiate their leadership behaviors by being directive or nondirective as the situation warrants (see Figure 3.9).

FIGURE 3.9

Leadership Responsibility Associated with Phase 4: Manage Personal Transitions

RESPONSIBILITY	CLASSROOM AND SCHOOL PRACTICES
Flexibility: *Adapts his or her leadership behavior to the needs of the current situation and is comfortable with dissent*	• Is comfortable with making major changes in how things are done • Encourages people to express diverse opinions contrary to those held by individuals in positions authority • Adapts leadership style to the needs of specific situations • Is directive or nondirective as the situation warrants

Being flexible includes understanding when to use authority to direct resources and to answer questions, as well as knowing when to step back, frame strategic questions, and encourage others to find answers. Principals must find the balance between setting direction for the school and listening to beliefs and opinions contrary to their own. Finally, principals must be comfortable with major changes in how things are done.

Often, principals may need to lead changes that are for themselves second-order changes. This requires that they engage in reflective practice and maintain an awareness of the implications of change for themselves and for others.

Poorly managed personal transitions are likely to exacerbate the feeling of loss that people may experience when engaged in what they view as second-order change. When people feel like they are losing something, they may look for someone to blame for their loss. The easiest person to blame in any organization is the one responsible for the change itself—in this case, the principal. For precisely this reason, change leadership can be a high-stakes proposition.

Monitoring and Evaluating Implementation

Purpose: This tool is designed to help school leaders plan for the Monitor and Evaluate phase of the change process.

Directions: Using the bundle of improvement efforts identified in Leadership Tool #4, determine how you plan to monitor and evaluate the implementation of the initiative, check for the impact of implementation on those doing the work, and attend to leading indicators.

1. Identify the specific actions you will take to fulfill the responsibility of *Monitor and Evaluate*.

2. Record the evidence you will collect to show that these actions were taken and their impact.

Monitoring and evaluating requires the leader to examine and determine the effectiveness of the implementation plan and the effect that the change is having on the stakeholders (magnitude of change)		
	What will you look for?	How and when will it be reported?
Implementation		
Magnitude of Change (e.g., the effect the change has on stakeholders)		

Tool #11 (p. 68) provides a guide for planning your approach to this challenging phase.

Recall that our follow-up study of research (the factor analysis) identified four leadership responsibilities—*Culture, Order, Communication,* and *Input*—that have a negative correlation to change with second-order implications. To effectively manage personal transitions, school leaders must share these responsibilities. Figure 3.10 provides examples of how a school leadership team or a designated transition team (e.g., school-level administrators, central office resource staff, teachers, parents, students, and other community members) might fulfill these responsibilities while the principal remains focused on the seven responsibilities positively linked to second-order change.

Overall, effective change leadership relies on understanding the change process, which includes connecting research-based leadership responsibilities with the phases of change.

Figure 3.11, p. 67, shows how the seven leadership responsibilities that have a positive correlation to leading change with second-order implications can be emphasized in each of the phases of change.

FIGURE 3.10
Responsibilities to Share with Your Leadership Team

Culture: *Fosters shared beliefs and a sense of community and cooperation*

The team helps articulate a vision or picture of where the school or program is heading. Team members help set up vicarious and mastery experiences that support acquisition of new knowledge and new skills and encourage positive attitudes. They focus on successes and interpret disappointments as opportunities for improvement. They help clarify parts that individuals can play in successfully implementing changes.

Order: *Establishes a set of standard operating procedures and routines*

The team plans and stages ceremonial events that honor the past and clarify what is ending and what is beginning. They develop or negotiate temporary agreements or policies to provide new structures to guide and support behavior as new norms emerge.

Communication: *Establishes strong lines of communication with and among teachers and students*

Team members listen to concerns about clarity of the plan for change, implementation of the plan, and needed support. They continually articulate the new direction of the organization, clarify and simplify when possible, help individuals see connections between shared values and aspirations and the new direction, and focus on the relative advantage of changes to everyone involved. They highlight short-term successes to feature evidence of impact as well as learning opportunities.

Input: *Involves teachers in the design and implementation of important decisions and policies*

The team encourages and actively seeks experiences of the staff with implementation. They plan and facilitate periodic study sessions to learn what is working, what is not working, and to reiterate the reasons or purpose for the change initiative.

FIGURE 3.11

How Leadership Responsibilities Relate to Phases of the Change Process

LEADERSHIP RESPONSIBILITIES	PHASES OF THE CHANGE PROCESS
Intellectual Stimulation: *Ensures faculty and staff are aware of the most current theories and practices and makes the discussion of these a regular aspect of the school's culture* **Change Agent:** *Is willing to challenge and actively challenges the status quo* **Ideals and Beliefs:** *Communicates and operates from strong ideals and beliefs about schooling*	**Create Demand:** A pervasive expectation of continuous improvement, regardless of perceived obstacles or limitation, contributes to a push for continuous improvement. Principals expose teachers to research and related information about effective practices, and then engage them in discussions about how to apply research findings in their classrooms. School leaders challenge the status quo, always considering new and better ways of doing things. Principals also keep themselves up-to-date on cutting-edge ideas about how to improve individual and school effectiveness. They routinely share beliefs about teaching and learning, modeling these beliefs through actions.
Knowledge of Curriculum, Instruction, and Assessment: *Is knowledgeable about current curriculum, instruction, and assessment practices* **Optimize:** *Inspires and leads new and challenging innovations*	**Implement:** Principals develop knowledge of effective, research-based curriculum, instruction, and assessment practices, and then use this knowledge to provide conceptual guidance to teachers. Principals inspire teachers to use demanding, research-based classroom practices; believe that teachers can successfully implement these practices; and convey this belief to them. Principals interpret disappointments in ways that help school staff see them as temporary and isolated, and interpret successes in ways that help staff view them as permanent and universal.
Monitor and Evaluate: *Monitors the effectiveness of school practices and their impact on student learning*	**Monitor and Evaluate:** There is real-time access to and use of all relevant data on needs and performance of individuals, groups, and the organization. Leadership pays attention to the quality of implementation of research-based instructional and classroom practices. Analyses of formative data on leading indicators of implementation and impact are fed into decisions about the pace and intensity of additional changes. Change implementation is carefully monitored.
Flexibility: *Adapts his or her leadership behavior to the needs of the current situation and is comfortable with dissent*	**Manage Personal Transitions:** The principal understands when to direct, when to step back, when to answer questions and when to ask them, when to speak and when to listen. He or she understands the fear and stress of second-order change for stakeholders. Leadership gives attention to the importance of symbolic events and a willingness to establish temporary agreements to assist those who need extra support. The principal makes clear the reasons for change, shares an attractive vision of what will be different because of the change, develops a change-management plan, and specifies the new roles, responsibilities, and activities for all stakeholders.

Managing Personal Transitions

Purpose: This tool is designed to help school leaders plan for the Manage Personal Transitions phase of the change process.

Directions:

1. Identify a change initiative tied to measurable student outcomes for your school.

2. Determine how you plan to differentiate your approach based on individual needs and create new structures and processes to do the work required of the new initiative.

3. Identify the specific actions you will take to fulfill the responsibility of Flexibility.

4. Record the evidence you will collect to show that these actions were taken and the impact they had.

In general, what do staff members stand to lose as a result of the change?
What are some preliminary strategies to assist staff members who will experience this initiative as second-order change?
Flexibility—How will you demonstrate, and show evidence of, *Flexibility*? Actions: Evidence:

CHAPTER 4

Creating a
Purposeful Community

John Parker and Janice Boyd are the principal and assistant principal of Evergreen Middle School in Spokane Valley, Washington, a school with a largely middle-class population and fast-changing demographics. Parker, a former "building manager" type of leader, and Boyd, who had experienced frustration as a teacher with such leaders, have combined their strengths to turn their school culture into one where *teachers* are the experts.

When Parker and Boyd came on board, 80 percent of the students at Evergreen were passing, and the general attitude among staff was "What's the problem?" But the new leadership—and the district—saw problems. Overall, students were doing pretty well, mostly because many of them have strong family support and access to resources; but test scores had flat-lined, achievement gaps among subgroups of students were growing, and the staff didn't share a common focus.

Simply stated, the school had reached a performance ceiling and breaking through it would likely require more consistent implementation of effective teaching practices—an arguably technical solution. However, if implementing a simple, straightforward solution was the only thing that needed to be done, the school probably would have done that a long time ago. The real break-through, Parker and Boyd reasoned, would come from finding new ways of working together, something more akin to an adaptive challenge.

Parker and Boyd, both trained in second-order change, were excited to get started. "As the building's new administrative team, I thought, here's our opportunity to get some structure around what our leadership might really look like," says Boyd.

They knew all about the practices that would positively affect the school culture and, ultimately, student achievement: clear learning objectives in every classroom; a living, breathing school improvement plan; regular meetings with staff to discuss student performance data; good communication with parents; high expectations for students. But they had to figure out how to apply those practices on a daily basis, creating shared accountability for doing what needed to be done. That's where the adaptive challenge would begin.

And they needed to get the staff on board. With several teachers who have been at the school for 10 years or longer and a handful near retirement, second-order change was especially hard. In the early going, Parker and Boyd estimated that only about half of the teachers were fully on board with the changes they wanted to make. The others were holding back, waiting for the latest wave of reform to pass over.

In their first couple of years at Evergreen, Parker and Boyd worked intensively with staff to help them understand the importance of creating a strong, collaborative culture. Then they shifted to examining classroom instructional practices and clearly defined learning objectives.

Their approach was gradual, a mix of patience and pressure. Parker, who is an even-keeled and matter-of-fact leader, firmly believes that everyone will come around eventually because "the data will speak for itself," he says. "There is no reason to rant and rave. Teachers get it; 95 to 97 percent of the time, they will come to the same conclusion about student performance."

Boyd echoes this belief, saying that they have worked hard to build trust with teachers. "Teachers have to know that I'm not passing judgment. This isn't about dinging them on their evaluations; it's really about how I can support them and their work."

The culture at Evergreen Middle School—and, Boyd believes, throughout education—is shifting away from a culture where teachers close their classroom doors to one where teachers must work together as professionals—much like a medical staff—to diagnose problems, develop treatments, and ensure that treatment protocols are followed consistently. "The best way to get at it is to challenge the teachers' thinking, to get them to really reflect."

Parker and Boyd hold regular conversations with the faculty about student performance. They make student achievement a regular topic of staff meetings. They keep the school improvement plans active and current. They talk with confidence about students and instruction—and the idea of how much better the school can perform. They envision and articulate better outcomes. They have "Collaboration Thursdays," during which staff focus squarely on improving teaching and learning. Parker and Boyd do regular informal classroom observations to look for critical teaching skills. The leadership team meets regularly, not twice a year, as it did before.

"Today I think we have pockets of success where some of our collaborative teams are working better than others," Parker says. But "teamwork ebbs and flows," he adds, for different reasons—personnel changes, an overload of administrative tasks, a new technology program, an upcoming new teacher evaluation process, and other district initiatives.

"I've learned over time that, regardless of what we're working on, I don't apologize for my teachers for who they are," says Parker. "So many people want teachers to be perfect. My philosophy is to take what I have and work with what I've got, and work together to get better. Do I have a couple of teachers who are pretty close to retiring and aren't really with the new program? Yes. Do I honor and respect them for what they've done in 35 years? Yes, I think it's important that I do that."

But that doesn't mean letting them off the hook. A team is, of course, only as strong as its weakest member. Parker and Boyd realized that creating a strong culture sometimes requires having difficult conversations. In recent years, a few teachers have been quietly and gently encouraged to find either another school or another profession. Each personnel action, Parker and Boyd understand, offers promise and peril—*promise* of opening up a spot for a more effective and enthusiastic teacher to join the team and *peril* of undermining the very esprit de corps Parker and Boyd are working hard to create. It's a bit of a paradox, Parker observes. On the one hand, "you are trying to get people to grow and have them be open, to be collegial, to listen to each other and point out their faults and be self-reflective." On the other hand, that very process might draw attention to faults and weaknesses that could prove their professional undoing.

In the end, creating a strong school culture and climate where people collaborate and work together with a fail-forward mindset yet remain results-oriented—holding one another and themselves accountable for continuous improvement—is, it turns out, another critical balancing act for school leaders. Although there's no step-by-step recipe for creating such a culture, there are key principles that can serve as guideposts for building a school culture that both supports teachers' professional growth and continuously challenges them to improve their practices—something we call a "purposeful community."

The Secret Sauce of School Success: A Culture of High Expectations

We've probably all experienced the feeling of walking into a high-performing school. Often there's something intangible in the air, something we can sense but not quite put our fingers on that tells us this place is different. Maybe it's the tidiness of the hallways. Perhaps it's the messages we see in the artwork and posters on the walls. Maybe it's the engagement we see in students' faces when we visit classrooms. Perhaps it's the seriousness that teachers bring to their jobs, even while connecting with students.

So what is this mysterious "it" that all successful schools seem to have, which we can detect but not always identify? As it turns out, research provides an answer.

Some years ago, a research team at McREL set out on a four-year study to determine how high-poverty, high-performing, "beat-the-odds" schools differ from low-performing schools in matched comparison studies (McREL, 2005). The team identified 739 high-performing and 738 low-performing schools with 50 percent or more of students in poverty and surveyed teachers in four key areas: (1) school environment, (2) professional community, (3) leadership, and (4) instruction. Teachers were, for example, asked to identify the level to which they agreed or disagreed with statements such as these:

- My school has an explicit statement of high expectations concerning student achievement.
- There is a safe, orderly learning environment in my school.
- Administrators, teachers, and parents share a common vision of school improvement.
- My students know their learning goals.

Some surprising differences emerged between the perceptions of teachers in the two groups—mostly in what those in low-performing schools said *wasn't* happening in their schools. Although they reported the presence of many of the "right" things, such as offering challenging curricula, encouraging teacher collaboration, and providing professional development, the missing ingredients—the things that beat-the-odds schools were attending to that were noticeably absent in struggling schools—appeared to add up to a different, and better, kind of school *culture* (see Figure 4.1). That such well-worn school reform components as assessment and monitoring, collaboration, professional development, and individualizing instruction didn't surface as distinguishing features doesn't mean they're unimportant. Teachers in high-performing schools said that these things *were* present in their schools. But so did teachers in low-performing schools, which suggests that such things aren't the *distinguishing* features of higher-performing schools.

What appeared to separate the beat-the-odds schools from others is that they had developed, with input from teachers, a common vision—which included helping all students meet high expectations for learning. Woven into the fabric of these schools was the belief that all students can learn—as well as a no-nonsense attitude about behavior, which translated into an orderly school climate and strong classroom management. Perhaps most notably, teachers reported having influence in school decisions—they shared the vision and owned the success of the school.

What all of this seems to add up to is that culture may well be the secret sauce of school improvement. Culture, as the saying goes, eats strategy for lunch. Low-performing schools, as researcher Charles Payne (2008) has noted, often behave like mentally depressed individuals, believing nothing they do can make a difference; the moment they encounter a roadblock,

FIGURE 4.1

Distinguishing Characteristics of Beat-the-Odds Schools

- **Shared mission and goals** (common vision and clear focus for resources)
- **Academic press for achievement** (high expectations for all)
- **Orderly climate** (clear and enforced rules for student behavior)
- **Structure** (clear student goals, strong classroom management)
- **Support for teacher influence** (leadership shared with teachers)

they throw their hands up in the air in defeat or start infighting and shifting blame. Indeed, in dysfunctional school environments, even the best-laid school improvement efforts—ones that borrow approaches that have worked in countless other settings—tend to fall flat. In contrast, high-performing schools pull together, not apart, in the face of adversity. They take good ideas and make them even better. And they challenge one another to get just a little bit better every day. Consider, for example, ongoing research from the Consortium on Chicago School Research, which compared the 30 most highly rated schools in Chicago with 30 of the lowest-performing schools and found that, in particular, the level of trust and respect teachers have for one another proved to be one of the best predictors of school performance (Payne, 2008).

In sum, one key to unlocking a better school culture, as noted above, is a shared sense of purpose and vision that focuses everyone on setting and achieving high expectations for student learning. Another key, as the following example illustrates, is not at all flashy. In fact, it's often as plain as plain vanilla can be.

Consistency:
Overcoming the "Forrest Gump" principle of school performance

Several years ago, school researcher Sam Stringfield had a mystery on his hands, one that eventually led him and his colleagues to piece together what the mysterious "it" in high-performing schools might be. Stringfield had found schools of similar size, context, and socioeconomic status in Louisiana and matched one high-performing school with one low-performing school. He then asked a group of observers, mostly lay people, to tour the schools, looking for clues as to what made them high-performing or low-performing. However, to ensure their observations remained unbiased, he did not tell the observers which schools were performing well and which were not. And yet, the observers were able to separate the princes from the frogs, so to speak, which initially puzzled Stringfield because the high-performing schools were hardly dazzling on the surface. In fact, many were as plain as could be imagined.

After poring over the data for a whole summer, he began to reach out to the observers to find out what had tipped them off. They came back with this answer: In the high-performing schools, they would walk into classroom after classroom and observe the same thing—teachers focused on teaching and students engaged in learning. In the low-performing schools, on the other hand, they saw no such consistency in classrooms. Sure, they could spot some great teachers doing outstanding work here and there, but in the classroom next door, they might find little teaching or learning going on. What Stringfield observed (Stringfield, Reynolds, & Schaffer, 2010) led us to suggest something we call the "Forrest Gump principle" of low-performing schools: Classrooms in low-performing schools are like a box of chocolates; you never know what you're going to get (Goodwin, 2011b). In contrast, teachers in high-performing schools appear to have a shared commitment to consistency, providing, in essence, a guarantee to students (and parents) that no matter what classroom they find themselves in, they'll have a high-quality learning experience. Providing such a guarantee, we've concluded, requires nothing flashy or exciting, but simply a whole-school commitment to consistently high-quality teaching.

Starting with a glass half full

Often educators, especially those in low-performing schools, lament what they do not have, complaining about too few resources, too little time, and students with deficits in social capital. Positive school cultures, however, tend to develop an entirely different mindset when it comes to resources. For example, the previously cited research on turnaround leaders (Public Impact, 2008) notes that these leaders focus their limited resources on where they'll have the greatest impact. They might ask, for example, what are we doing with our paraprofessionals? Are they engaged in one-on-one tutoring with students, which research shows to be one of the most effective ways to improve student learning (U.S. Department of Education, 2009), or are they making photocopies?

A study of school districts in four states found a positive correlation between resources and student achievement, but also a distinctly different pattern of spending in high-performing, rapidly improving districts than in low-performing ones—namely, directing the limited resources they had toward instructional programs and away from administrative functions and administrative staff (Pan, Rudo, Schneider, & Smith-Hansen, 2003). Moreover, these higher-performing districts did not let perceived obstacles, such as restrictions on allocating categorical funds, stand in the way of directing resources to where they were most needed; rather, they treated them as resolvable challenges.

When it comes to time, the pessimist's refrain is that there's just too little of it; we only see students a small fraction of their lives, so how we can be expected to have much impact on them? The reality, though, is that much of the precious time students spend in school is lost to nonlearning activities. When you subtract the time for things like recess, lunch, classroom management, as well as classroom time off-task, it would appear that students only spend about 42 percent of their day at school engaged in actual learning (Martella, Nelson, & Marchand-Martella, 2003). Good schools do not accept this loss of time as a fait accompli. A study of 30 schools that have been successful in serving high-needs students found that one of the common themes is that they take time seriously—from how much time they devote to academic versus nonacademic activities to how well they use time in the classroom (National Center on Time and Learning, 2011).

Perhaps the biggest key here is that these high-performing schools operate not from a deficit model—one that dwells on what they don't have, or the limitations, obstacles, and shortcomings of their circumstances—but rather from an asset model that views the glass as half full. This attitude often starts with views toward the students themselves—for example, instead of dwelling on perceived deficits in students' so-called social capital, these schools recognize and build upon many of the strengths that students of color bring to school, including aspirations, bilingualism, extended families, and resilience (Yosso, 2005).

Boston Public Schools has engaged in a districtwide effort to incorporate asset-based thinking into their approach to instruction as well as professional development. Teachers were shown how to build lessons around students' strengths so that each student could be both challenged and successful in the learning experience. At the same time, teacher-coaches observed classrooms for examples of teachers using effective practices and encouraged them to employ those practices with even greater frequency. The Boston educators noted that the approach marked a major, positive cultural shift in how teachers and students interacted with one another, and an independent evaluation found that it showed promise in raising student achievement, especially for 10th grade students who demonstrated significant improvements in learning (Paek, 2008).

In sum, the culture of successful schools focuses not on weaknesses or deficits, but rather seeks to use what resources are available as wisely as possible and build on strengths. This approach reflects what Gallup researchers cite as the foundation of a strengths-based organization—one that assumes each person has "enduring and unique" talents and "each person's greatest room for growth is in the areas of his or her greatest strength" (Buckingham & Clifton, 2001, p. 7).

The power of "can do"

A final key to developing a strong school culture has its origins in a failed experiment conducted decades ago at the University of Pennsylvania. The researcher, who was following in the footsteps of Pavlov and would later become internationally famous, was hoping to see if dogs might become conditioned to a particular tone when it was followed by a mild electrical shock (akin to a static shock) and exhibit automatic response, reacting with fear at the sound of the tone. After conditioning the dogs to the pairing of the tone with the shock, he placed them in a large box with two compartments separated by a low wall between them so that the dogs (German Shepherds) could easily jump over to avoid the shock. He expected that when he rang the tone, the dogs would jump into the adjoining compartment. Instead, the dogs cowered and whimpered, making no attempt to avoid the coming jolts of electricity.

The researcher, Martin Seligman (1990), concluded that the dogs had been "taught" to be helpless. During the conditioning, nothing they did changed the outcome (they got shocked every time); thus, they "learned that nothing they did mattered. So why try?" (p. 20). Observing the dogs' "learned helplessness," he realized that downtrodden people often exhibit similar behavior, which launched him on a 20-year quest to determine how a person's prevailing outlook on life—optimistic or pessimistic—leads to different choices and outcomes.

Since that time, researchers have found that entire groups of people can develop a similar kind of learned helplessness. Consider low-performing schools. Teachers in these schools often come to believe that nothing ever gets better and nothing they do matters, so they hunker down and wait for each new program or reform to pass. In such demoralized school cultures, even the simplest technical solution—such as bringing in a new reading program, creating 90-minute reading blocks, or extending the school day—often has little impact. Some teachers may ignore the solutions; others may try them but give up the moment they encounter a setback. Only a few soldier on, but their efforts become so isolated that they have little overall effect.

In contrast, teachers in successful schools set a high bar for themselves and their students; they believe that as individuals and a group, they are capable of improving student achievement—something researchers call "collective efficacy," which is a *shared perception or belief* held by a group that they can organize and execute a course of action that makes a difference (Goddard, 2001). Moreover, they trust their colleagues to work as hard as they do to make it happen. Wayne Hoy and his colleagues (Hoy, Tarter, & Hoy, 2006) have labeled this mix of dispositions *academic optimism* and have found it to be a more powerful predictor of student achievement than students' socioeconomic status.

In schools with high levels of collective efficacy, teachers believe that, together, they can positively affect student achievement (Goddard, Hoy, & Hoy, 2004). When collective efficacy is positive and strong, and academics are emphasized, teachers are more likely to persist in the face of challenges.

A meta-analysis of research on effective leaders (Marzano, Waters, & McNulty, 2005) points to the importance of building a "can-do" school culture. Among the 21 responsibilities of school leaders linked to higher levels of student achievement, the research found that effective principals do the following:

- Set high, concrete goals and expectations for all students to reach those goals. (Focus)

- Develop a clear vision for what the school could be like and promote a sense of staff cooperation and cohesion. (Culture)

- Involve teachers in decision making and sharing leadership. (Input)

- Systematically celebrate teachers' accomplishments. (Affirmation)

The Four Characteristics of a Purposeful Community

So let's put these ideas together. First, we've seen from research that beat-the-odds schools develop a *culture of high expectations* with a common vision and sense of ownership of where the school is going. Second, we've seen that one of the most distinguishable characteristics of high-performing schools is that they achieve *consistency* from classroom to classroom, avoiding the box-of-chocolate surprises. Third, they use that vision and shared purpose to focus their resources on doing what matters most for students and operate not from a deficit model, but rather by using *asset-based thinking* about resources. Fourth, they demonstrate a strong *can-do spirit*, or sense of collective efficacy. Put it all together and you get what we characterize as a "purposeful community," which is composed of these four elements:

- A strong sense of moral purpose and high expectations (*purpose and outcomes that matter to all*)

- A shared commitment to consistency (*agreed-upon processes*)

- Focusing resources on what matters most and building on strengths (*use of all available assets*)

- A prevailing sense of optimism and a can-do attitude (*collective efficacy*)

The key idea here is that, as a community develops and sustains these characteristics, it becomes increasingly purposeful—everything the school does, it does with the intent of creating a culture of continuous improvement and helping students succeed. School culture—positive or negative—starts with leadership, making school principals perhaps the most important players in shaping the culture of the school. Creating a purposeful community is not easy, but as we'll show in the following sections, it can be done. As a first step, you can use Tool #12 to assess where you are on your journey to creating a purposeful community.

Creating purpose and outcomes that matter to all

Recall that the teachers we surveyed in beat-the-odds schools reported having greater influence in school decisions than teachers in low-performing schools. This situation requires leaders to invite teachers into dialogue to develop a vision of meaningful outcomes that they can only achieve as a community. Simply stated, leaders help community members answer the following question: What is it that we can only do because we are together as a community that we cannot do as individuals?

An important first step in creating conditions that invite people to become part of a purposeful community is to create an environment that is psychologically safe and encourages people to share their beliefs, assumptions, philosophies, and values in order to discover shared purposes and outcomes for the school community. Heifetz and Linsky (2002) suggest that leaders create "holding environments," or "safe places," where all members of the school community can talk about what is going on in the organization, voice dissent and raise objections, be hard on ideas (but not on one another), and openly discuss assumptions. Holding environments not only help stakeholders tackle difficult issues in a productive way, but also make it possible for people to voice emotional or troubling concerns in a more productive manner. Some examples of holding environments include structured dialogues, protocols, strategic questioning, study groups, and focus groups. Creating holding environments is an acquired skill and requires practice. At first, these structures may seem unnatural and can be difficult to sustain. However, if used as intended, holding environments promote productive interactions that support collaboration and collegiality.

Developing agreed-upon processes

The consistency in classroom practice that Sam Stringfield found in high-performing schools doesn't occur by accident (Stringfield, Reynolds, & Schaffer, 2010). It's the product of teachers working together with school leaders to ensure a high bar for professional practice in every classroom. This collaboration requires trust among staff members and an openness to peer coaching, critical feedback, and continuous improvement. Stated differently, members of the school community must agree on how they work together by establishing agreed-upon processes that support effective patterns of communication, strong relationships among community members, a sense of individual well-being, meaningful connections between the school and other institutions important to schools (such as local libraries, universities, and

Purposeful Community: Teacher's Reflection Assessment

Purpose: This tool is designed to help school leaders determine the level of purposeful community currently existing in their school community.

Directions:

1. Ask teachers to read each statement and evaluate the extent to which they think your school exhibits each of these qualities.

2. Tally the responses from teachers and share the results with the staff.

The gray boxes indicate our view of an ideal purposeful community. Compare your perceptions of your school with the description of the ideal purposeful community description. The areas where your responses differ from the ideal suggest areas for improvement as you develop and maintain a purposeful community at your school. By reflecting on your perceptions, your perceptions of your staff's responses, and the actual responses of your staff, you can identify the characteristics of purposeful community that need additional consideration.

PURPOSEFUL COMMUNITY: TEACHER'S REFLECTION TOOL	1 NOT AT ALL	2	3	4 TO A GREAT EXTENT
PURPOSE AND OUTCOMES				
1. School outcomes have the same meaning for all teachers.				▓
2. Teachers here share the same purpose.				▓
3. Teachers in this school all agree on their purpose.				▓
4. Teachers here think individual goals equal a common school goal.	▓			
AGREED-UPON PROCESSES				
5. The lack of procedures for communicating makes problem solving difficult.	▓			
6. Teachers in this school identify obstacles that interfere with the school's purpose.				▓
7. Teachers here are in consensus on ways of working together.				▓
8. Teachers in this school do not have personal connections with each other.	▓			
USE OF ALL AVAILABLE ASSETS				
9. Teachers in this school regularly review asset allocation.				▓
10. Teachers in this school effectively use assets to increase the impact of classroom practices.				▓

(continued)

PURPOSEFUL COMMUNITY: TEACHER'S REFLECTION TOOL

	1	2	3	4
	NOT AT ALL ⟶ TO A GREAT EXTENT			
11. The intangible resources available in this school are difficult to measure.	▓			
12. Leaders here capitalize on intangible assets.				▓
COLLECTIVE EFFICACY				
13. Teachers in this school are able to get through to difficult students.				▓
14. Teachers here are confident they will be able to motivate their students.				▓
15. Teachers in this school really believe every child can learn.				▓
16. If a child doesn't want to learn, teachers here give up.	▓			
17. Teachers here don't have the skills needed to produce meaningful student learning.	▓			
18. These students come to school ready to learn.			▓	
19. Home life provides so many advantages the students here are bound to learn.			▓	
20. Students here just aren't motivated to learn.	▓			
21. The opportunities in this community help ensure that these students will learn.				▓
22. Learning is more difficult at this school because students are worried about their safety.	▓			
23. Drug and alcohol abuse in the community make learning difficult for students here.	▓			
24. Teachers in this school do not have the skills to deal with student disciplinary problems.	▓			

Note: The overall instrument (24 items) has not been validated, limiting its range of uses. However, information from a comprehensive literature review was used to generate the items. The items are well aligned to the theories presented in the literature, so there is some content validity evidence for their inclusion. Because validity evidence has not been collected for the overall tool, it should not be used diagnostically or to provide summative judgments about the school. Items 13–24, intended to measure collective efficacy, represent the work of Goddard, Hoy, and Hoy (2000) and Goddard (2002) (reprinted with permission). Extensive validity studies have been conducted on these items as a stand-alone survey.

businesses), shared leadership, and a sense of order and discipline. When necessary, agreed-upon processes provoke the community into action, especially when the status quo is not moving the community toward achieving its purposes. When instability, rather than stability, is needed, revisiting a school's agreed-upon processes is warranted. Determining what new agreements are needed and challenging the community to examine current realities in light of a preferred future are important ways that leadership produces the energy necessary to move in a new direction.

Agreed-upon processes in a purposeful community include two elements: operating principles and agreements. *Operating principles* form the identity of an organization and provide guidance to its members. Every organization, including your school, has operating principles. In the best sense, they lay the foundation for how individuals will function in the community. Operating principles are either implicit, in that they are present but not formally discussed, or explicit, in which case the members of the organization have an opportunity to discuss and agree upon them. Making operating principles explicit and visible allows the staff to examine them and decide whether they are consistent with the established mission and goals. *Agreements* are the overtly stated ways of working that a group identifies and adopts to exemplify the principles that community members value. They are the formal and informal policies and practices that create behavioral expectations for members of the purposeful community. They bring the operating principles to daily life in the organization. Agreements relate to behaviors or actions, and they can change. Agreements also define what living by an operating principle requires of members of the community. You can use Tool #13 to help you identify and clarify your school's operating principles and associated agreements.

Developing and using all available assets

As noted earlier, successful schools employ asset-based thinking, making the most of their existing resources to reach their goals by building on existing strengths. Doing so requires intentional leaders (Kaplan & Norton, 2004) who understand the importance of and the difference between intangible assets.

Tangible assets have a physical existence and are easily measured. In a school setting, some examples include funding, personnel, technology, annual reports, and strategic plans. These are usually assets that leaders think of when asked about what makes their jobs easier. Though important, tangible assets alone do not guarantee greater productivity or increased student achievement. The key is to ensure that tangible assets are tightly aligned to outcomes that matter.

Intangible assets, although difficult to measure and easily overlooked, can be just as important as tangible assets. In a school setting, some examples

Developing Operating Principles and Agreements

Purpose: This tool is intended to help school leaders identify and define the operating principles and agreements that should be in place in order to move toward their purpose and outcomes that matter.

Directions:

1. Capture and organize the key topics, ideas, and statements that resulted from asking the members of the community, "What can we accomplish only by working together?"

2. Select 3–5 of the most prevalent ideas that were captured from the "outcomes that matter to all" conversations.

3. Identify an operating principle your school needs if your purposeful community is truly committed to reaching this outcome.

4. To identify specific agreements that must be in place for all community members to live by the defined operating principle, use the sentence stem "[Select operating principle] requires of us that we _____."

STATEMENTS FROM PURPOSE AND OUTCOMES CONVERSATIONS	OPERATING PRINCIPLE AND DEFINITION	AGREEMENTS THE OPERATING PRINCIPLE,_____ REQUIRES OF US THAT WE _____ _____ .

are shared vision, trust, reputation, and optimism. Intangible assets help to form a school's identity. Leaders who spend time identifying and leveraging intangibles are more likely to maximize those assets and produce intended outcomes (Low & Kalafut, 2002; Ulrich & Smallwood, 2004). Here are a few key steps to develop a plan for using intangible assets:

- Define the intangible assets that are important in your school.

- Inventory the intangible assets that currently exist in your school or district by collecting perception data about what staff members and other stakeholders see as strengths of your school, including their own individual talents and strengths.

- Consider how to build on these strengths and intangible assets in your school improvement planning.

The following tools (Tools #14 and #15) will help you assess how your school currently uses intangible assets and uncover the tangible and intangible assets your staff offers.

Developing and sustaining collective efficacy

The final aspect of purposeful community is a shared can-do attitude, or sense of collective efficacy. It is important to note that collective efficacy, like individual self-efficacy, is task-specific. In other words, a school faculty may have a high degree of collective efficacy regarding their collective ability to teach all students to read but not in their collective ability to raise student achievement in mathematics. Collective efficacy is greater when faculty members perceive their colleagues as competent in using instructional strategies and, conversely, diminished when faculty members perceive their colleagues as incompetent, particularly in curricular or instructional areas. Research by Hoy, Smith, and Sweetland (2002) shows that

- The more efficacious a school is, the more likely that school is to accept and embrace challenging goals. When staff members believe they can overcome challenges, they are more likely to step up and accept them, even when the challenges seem insurmountable.

- Efficacious schools put forth more effort. This effort may be displayed in establishing and sustaining study groups, observing colleagues, and collectively reviewing student work.

- Efficacious schools understand the benefit of persistence. Teachers in these schools do not give up when the going gets tough. Rather, they dig deeper, band together, and push through adversity, knowing that eventually, based on their efforts, they will succeed.

As you might imagine, developing and sustaining collective efficacy in a school has implications for school leaders. Research provides guidance on how to constructively nurture and sustain collective efficacy, including specific

Assessing Use of Intangible Assets

Purpose: This tool is designed to help school leaders determine the degree to which intangible assets represent a focus for their school.

Directions: For each element, place an X in the box following the description that best describes how your school is currently using its intangible assets.

Tip: For any of the characteristics you have marked as "somewhat effective" or "least effective," identify what you would need to do to improve your school's use of intangible assets.

LEAST EFFECTIVE	SOMEWHAT EFFECTIVE	MOST EFFECTIVE
DEFINING/IDENTIFYING INTANGIBLE ASSETS		
Intangible assets are not a regular part of conversations about leadership and school improvement. Intangible assets are not formally identified. ☐	There are informal conversations about which intangible assets might be most important to the school. Informal attempts are made to identify the intangible assets and strengths that exist in the school and how they are used. ☐	Intangible assets are studied. The most important assets and strengths for improving the school have been identified and agreed upon. An audit of intangible assets has been conducted. ☐
PLANNING		
The school improvement process does not explicitly focus on intangible assets or existing strengths. Decision-making and problem-solving approaches focus on tangible assets and deficits only. ☐	The school improvement process informally accounts for intangible assets and strengths by incorporating perception data. Leaders address the research-based leadership responsibilities of culture, communication, and relationships. ☐	The school improvement process formally accounts for the impact of intangible assets and existing strengths. Intangible assets and strengths are identified and aligned with school improvement initiatives. ☐
USING INTANGIBLE ASSETS		
Intangible assets are used informally through some discussions of the strengths that individuals bring to the school. ☐	Intangible assets are used informally and address both individual strengths and a collective focus. ☐	A process for using and strengthening intangible assets is in place. Decision-making and problem-solving approaches include a focus on intangible assets. ☐

Identifying Staff Expertise

Purpose: This tool is designed to help school leaders discover the tangible and intangible assets represented by school staff members.

Directions:

1. Ask each staff member to complete this questionnaire.

2. Compile the data into a document and distribute a copy to each staff member.

Tip: You might conduct a similar survey with parents and other organizations in your school community.

Teacher _____ Grade level and subject:_____

1. Please describe your areas of expertise. Include areas in which you have a lot of knowledge and other skills, such as organizing or facilitating groups.

2. What languages do you speak and understand?

3. Do you have areas of cultural competence, including experience with other cultures?

4. What are your hobbies and interests?

5. List networks and alliances that you belong to, including contacts with community or business organizations.

6. What kinds of relevant life experiences and wisdom are you willing to share?

7. Can you offer professional development opportunities to others? Please explain.

actions leaders can take. Leaders can draw upon four sources of efficacy identified by Bandura (1997): (1) mastery experiences, (2) vicarious experiences, (3) social persuasion, and (4) affective states.

Mastery experiences. Efficacy increases when people experience initial success and have opportunities to build on these successes. Establishing conditions for "early wins" and building on these experiences reinforces group beliefs. For example, when teachers collaborate to learn instructional strategies and use those strategies with students who then show evidence of increased learning, their collective efficacy increases.

Vicarious experiences. Efficacy can also be strengthened when individuals and groups have the opportunity to observe successful individuals in situations with similar circumstances. When teachers see success, particularly in settings similar to their own, they begin to believe that they, too, can be successful. For example, two high schools with similar student demographics might decide to use vocabulary strategies to increase the background knowledge of their students. In each school, teachers attend training sessions to learn specific ways to use the vocabulary strategies. Upon implementation, one school intentionally uses the strategies, but the other school's implementation is spotty. When the second school sees the benefit of the intentional efforts in the first school, it schedules a day to observe. The vicarious experience helps the teachers in the second school see specific ways to implement the vocabulary strategies, which they then employ.

Social persuasion. This source of efficacy is also referred to as "normative press." Influential individuals within a group create high expectations and provide encouragement and support to others to persist in the pursuit of desired outcomes. The most effective social persuasion, however, is not coercive. Rather, teachers see their peers working hard and having success with the strategies they are using. With adequate support, such as professional development, team planning time, and opportunities to give and receive feedback, they begin to make necessary changes and persevere. As the saying goes, actions speak louder than words. One caveat: This type of experience is most effective in a building that is relatively cohesive; the more dissension there is among staff members, the less likely social persuasion will work.

Affective states. A shared sense of hope and optimism that the group can accomplish their desired outcomes, even after disappointments, is another key source of collective efficacy. As soon as you walk into some buildings, you can tell the emotional state of the organization by the interactions that you have with individuals. Controlling the level of stress in an organization influences that organization's affective state. The better the stress is managed, the better the chances are that collective efficacy will improve. However, controlling the affective state by reducing the level of stress does not mean that the organization should not confront difficult issues. As in our personal lives, this is akin to denial and will prove unproductive. In the end, avoiding difficult issues undermines collective efficacy.

Leading Toward a More Purposeful Community

A purposeful community develops largely as a result of its leadership. We identified 8 of the 21 leadership responsibilities that principals should emphasize to develop a purposeful community. Figure 4.2 provides guidance for translating these responsibilities into specific and potentially measurable indicators of purposeful communities. In addition, you can use Tool #16 (p. 89) to clarify your own thinking about how the leadership responsibilities relate to creating a purposeful community.

Optimism and leadership

In his research on learned optimism, Martin Seligman (1990) notes that people's explanatory style is crucial to whether they demonstrate learned optimism or pessimism. Do they view, for example, a disappointing result as a temporary setback or as a permanent reflection of their inadequacies? Similarly, do they see failure as a reflection that *everything* must be wrong, or do they look for bright spots and strengths on which to build even in the midst of defeat and disappointment? The less permanent and universal their interpretation of events, the more hope and optimism people display and the less likely they are to view a situation as hopeless or themselves as helpless.

In organizations, leaders who help people interpret setbacks as temporary and identify specific causes for resolving them also help staff develop a greater sense of collective efficacy. In short, if leaders model a positive explanatory style, they can inspire staff to do the same. Thus it's important for leaders to recognize not only how they explain successes, but also—and perhaps more important—how they interpret failures. Do they ascribe declining performance to external (or universal) factors over which people have no control (e.g., changing demographics of their school population)? If so, they will likely encourage learned helplessness, telling people their actions are futile. If, on the other hand, they look for specific causes for the problem (e.g., not providing adequate early interventions for reading), they can support greater learned optimism and, in turn, collective efficacy. Tool #17 (p. 90) provides a framework for using the leadership responsibilities to help develop a sense of optimism.

Balancing and sharing leadership

By this point, doing everything we've recommended in this book will likely seem overwhelming. You might be asking yourself, given that first-order and second-order change are seen through the eyes of individuals, How am I supposed to be more directive with one group of stakeholders and, at the

FIGURE 4.2
Developing a More Purposeful Community Through Leadership

LEADERSHIP RESPONSIBILITIES	CHARACTERISTICS OF PURPOSEFUL COMMUNITIES
Culture: *Fosters shared beliefs and a sense of community and cooperation* **Ideals and Beliefs:** *Communicates and operates from strong ideals and beliefs about schooling*	• There is consensus on reasons for working together, with general agreement on why the community exists, what can only be accomplished because its members are together as a community, and that they can accomplish what is important to them. • The principal promotes cooperation, a sense of well-being, and cohesion among the staff. • There is a shared understanding of purpose and a vision of what the school could be like. • The principal holds and shares strong beliefs about teaching, learning, and the capability of the community to accomplish specific outcomes, and demonstrates behaviors that are consistent with his or her espoused beliefs.
Communication: *Establishes strong lines of communication with and among teachers and students* **Visibility:** *Has quality contact and interactions with teachers and students*	• There are critical connections among key members of the community. • The principal is easily accessible to teachers, other staff, students, and community members. • The principal uses systematic and frequent visits to classrooms and elsewhere within the school, and presence in the community, to reinforce the importance of learning and the community's capability of accomplishing outcomes that matter.
Input: *Involves teachers in the design and implementation of important decisions*	• Leadership is widely shared throughout the community. Rather than being seen as a position and defined only through positional authority, it becomes everyone's responsibility, and all community members have opportunities to lead. • The principal reinforces this density of leadership by providing opportunities for input on all important decisions. • Leadership density is also increased through the development and use of a leadership team.
Relationships: *Demonstrates awareness of the personal aspects of teachers and staff* **Situational Awareness:** *Is aware of the details and the undercurrents in the running of the school and uses this information to address current and potential problems*	• Consensus is developed on ways of working together that reflect the "agreed-upon processes" that characterize purposeful communities. • These agreements are a product of the human and personal connections created by remaining aware of personal needs, staying informed about significant issues in the lives of community members, and acknowledging significant events in their lives. • These connections allow the principal to stay informed about relationships among groups and issues that might not surface on their own, and they contribute to the principal's ability to predict what could go wrong from day to day.
Affirmation: *Recognizes and celebrates school accomplishments and acknowledges failures*	• Recognizing the importance of balance, attention is given to building on strengths as well as addressing weaknesses, because such strengths are among the community's most important assets. • The principal systematically and fairly recognizes and celebrates accomplishments of teachers, staff, and students. The principal is also willing to acknowledge failures, which are viewed as learning opportunities. • The principal reinforces and builds on the individual strengths of all community members.

Using Leadership Responsibilities to Strengthen Purposeful Community

Purpose: This tool is designed to help school leaders solidify their understanding of purposeful community and the associated leadership responsibilities.

Directions:

1. Think about how you might lead your school community in becoming more purposeful.

2. For each of the characteristics of a purposeful community, select three leadership responsibilities that you could use to assist you in strengthening that characteristic of purposeful community.

Tip: You may want to use a journal to capture your thoughts about using leadership responsibilities to strengthen purposeful community in your school.

OUTCOMES THAT MATTER TO ALL

Leadership Responsibilities:

1. _____

2. _____

3. _____

USE OF ALL AVAILABLE ASSETS

Leadership Responsibilities:

1. _____

2. _____

3. _____

AGREED-UPON PROCESSES

Leadership Responsibilities:

1. _____

2. _____

3. _____

COLLECTIVE EFFICACY

Leadership Responsibilities:

1. _____

2. _____

3. _____

Interpreting Events Through the Leadership Responsibilities

Purpose: This tool is designed to help school leaders reflect on how they can respond to and interpret events in a manner that models optimism.

Directions:

1. Reflect on a recent event that was viewed negatively or positively by members of your school community.

2. Identify the leadership responsibilities that were important for you to emphasize as a part of the response to the event.

3. In Column 3, record how you used, or could have used, the responsibilities to respond to the event.

RESPONSIBILITIES	ACTIONS	USING THE RESPONSIBILITIES TO INTERPRET SUCCESSES AND FAILURES
Affirmation	Recognizes and celebrates school accomplishments and acknowledges failures	
Change Agent	Is willing to challenge and actively challenges the status quo	
Communication	Establishes strong lines of communication with and among teachers and students	
Contingent Rewards	Recognizes and rewards individual accomplishments	
Culture	Fosters shared beliefs and a sense of community and cooperation	
Discipline	Protects teachers from issues and influences that would detract from their teaching time or focus	
Flexibility	Adapts his or her leader-ship behavior to the needs of the current situation and is comfortable with dissent	
Focus	Establishes clear goals and keeps those goals in the forefront of the school's attention	
Ideals and Beliefs	Communicates and operates from strong ideals and beliefs about schooling	
Input	Involves teachers in the design and implementation of important decisions and policies	

RESPONSIBILITIES	ACTIONS	USING THE RESPONSIBILITIES TO INTERPRET SUCCESSES AND FAILURES
Intellectual Stimulation	Ensures that the faculty and staff are aware of the most current theories and practices and makes the discussion of these a regular aspect of the school culture	
Involvement in Curriculum, Instruction, and Assessment	Is directly involved in the design and implementation of curriculum, instruction, and assessment practices	
Knowledge of Curriculum, Instruction, and Assessment	Is knowledgeable about current curriculum, instruction, and assessment practices	
Monitor and Evaluate	Monitors the effectiveness of school practices and their impact on student learning	
Optimize	Inspires and leads new and challenging innovations	
Order	Establishes a set of standard operating procedures and routines	
Relationships	Demonstrates awareness of the personal aspects of teachers and staff	
Outreach	Is an advocate and spokesperson for the school to all stakeholders	
Resources	Provides teachers with materials and professional development necessary for the successful execution of their jobs	
Situational Awareness	Is aware of the details and the undercurrents in the running of the school and uses this information to address current and potential problems	
Visibility	Has quality contact and interactions with teachers and students	

same time, be more supportive with another, all around the same change initiative? How can one person do it all—keeping a school focused, differentiating leadership style according to the kind of change underway and people's perceptions of it, while building a purposeful community?

The simple answer to that question is that you cannot.

You need to share leadership. By sharing leadership, we do not mean abdicating your responsibility. All 21 leadership responsibilities came from the research on principals, and each is correlated to increased student achievement. Thus our guidance is that school leaders must become skillful at all of them. However, that does not mean that some of these responsibilities should not be shared. In fact, we would argue that when change has second-order implications for many in the school community, sharing these responsibilities is essential.

When you share leadership responsibilities among members of your school community, the community not only becomes stronger and more effective, but leadership capacity increases—quite simply because more people become responsible for leading the school. Tool #18 will help you—and, we hope, the other members of your leadership team who are reading this book with you—identify ways to share leadership so that it does not feel quite so lonely at the top.

Snapshot: Evergreen Middle School

When we set out to profile Evergreen principal John Parker for this book, he insisted that we also interview his assistant principal, Janice Boyd, with whom he shares leadership of the school. The two, in fact, were installed in their positions together, with the explicit charge from Terrie VanderWegen, Central Valley School District's assistant superintendent for teaching and learning, to change the school: the culture, the attitude, the instruction.

"How are we going to make this shift?" VanderWegen wondered, recalling that in Parker and Boyd's first few months "they were getting some real pushback because they were calling teachers on things we were asking them to point out." But the pair kept at it, driving home the need to create a purposeful community and build collective efficacy. By the second year, teachers began to see that "these guys are serious."

Eventually, by working in collaboration with an extended leadership team, Parker and Boyd turned the school improvement plan into a living, breathing document, which "has provided that whole collaborative team approach," according to Parker, providing the school with an increasingly "unified front" focused on achieving high expectations for all students.

Reflection on Shared Leadership

Purpose: This tool is designed to help school leaders explore the current reality of shared leadership in their school community by reviewing the eight leadership responsibilities associated with purposeful community, plus the leadership responsibility of Optimize.

Directions:

1. With your leadership team or in a meeting with your entire staff, complete the template by writing examples of the practices you use to fulfill each responsibility.

2. From your responses in Column 3, identify your strengths as a leadership team or staff.

3. From your responses in Column 3, identify the challenges your team faces in sharing leadership and discuss how you might address these challenges.

RESPONSIBILITIES	PRACTICES	EXAMPLES OF HOW YOU SHARE LEADERSHIP
Affirmation	Recognizes and celebrates school accomplishments and acknowledges failures	
Communication	Establishes strong lines of communication with and among teachers and students	
Culture	Fosters shared beliefs and a sense of community and cooperation	
Ideals and Beliefs	Communicates and operates from strong ideals and beliefs about schooling	
Input	Involves teachers in the design and implementation of important decisions and policies	
Optimize	Inspires and leads new and challenging innovations	
Relationships	Demonstrates awareness of the personal aspects of teachers and staff	
Situational Awareness	Is aware of the details and the undercurrents in the running of the school and uses this information to address current and potential problems	
Visibility	Has quality contact and interactions with teachers and students	

When we first profiled Evergreen Middle School in 2013, we observed significant gaps between the achievement of higher-income and lower-income students. On an eight-point scale in the state of Washington's achievement index, Evergreen's general student population scored on average three points higher than low-income students. One year later, that gap had shrunk to a 2.19-point gap.

Ensuring high-quality instruction in every classroom has become the new way of operating. "I think we are getting to a tipping point," Parker says. "It's how we do things."

CHAPTER 5

Conclusion: Characteristics of Great School Leaders

The job of school leadership has not gotten any easier since our initial studies a decade ago. In fact, it could be argued that ever-changing social, political, and economic landscapes make the role even more difficult. Principals are being asked to do more with less and with an ever-changing student population that brings new strengths—and new challenges. Not surprisingly, the turnover rate among school leaders remains high, along with the stress levels of those who remain in the job.

We hope, though, that the insights we've shared in this book about how to lead effectively can make the job just a little easier. Moreover, for leaders suffering from self-doubt about whether they're the right person for the job, it's worth noting that the process of interviewing a half dozen principals who had taken up the ideas from Balanced Leadership and applied them in their schools led us to another important insight: These successful leaders were all very different. Some were gregarious, extroverted, and charismatic. Others were reserved and quiet, but strong leaders nonetheless. Some seemed to have always aspired to a leadership role; others seemed drawn into it over time.

But none said they were outstanding leaders their first day on the job. All of them worked hard to become better leaders. That's an important point to which we'll return in a moment.

We also observed, however, that in some deep ways, these leaders had a few important characteristics in common. They're the kind of characteristics that do not readily show up in a scientific study or a quantitative meta-analysis. Rather, they appear to surface slowly, during after-school conversations with a principal in his office, or by observing her interacting with teachers and students on the job.

Deep Conviction and Moral Purpose

Deep down in the successful principals we met, we found an abiding sense of moral purpose. For Mike Andersen, it was a conviction that your fate is not chosen for you as an individual and that education helps students alter their lives and control their own destinies. "What are we about?" asks Andersen. "What do we believe? Why are we here in this school and what are we doing to make it a better place for students? If we don't know the answer to those questions, we shouldn't be here."

George Boser, another principal who had applied Balanced Leadership principles in his school, Sedalia Elementary in Douglas County, Colorado, told us that it was his desire to pay it forward—to have the same kind of impact on others' lives that a teacher had had on his—that drew him to the principalship. Boser grew up poor in small towns in Iowa and Kansas. By the time he reached early adolescence, he was decidedly nonconformist in many ways, including how he viewed his own school leaders. Despite professing how much they cared about all students, he saw the adults in the schools he attended—and later, in schools where he worked—judging him on his appearance and, specifically, his earrings and tattoos. "I saw a lot of hypocrisy. I remember, all the way back to 6th grade, feeling that this was wrong. It seemed like there was always a teacher taking a shot at me, for whatever reason. I thought, 'You are going to judge me on the outside—that's what you are telling me, as an adult?' I knew it wasn't right."

Then, as a junior in high school in Council Grove, Kansas, Boser had a teacher who seemed to open the world to a larger view, urging students to take a hard look at the civil rights movement in the United States, at apartheid in South Africa, about "caring for humans—real stuff. He brought in the truth behind it. He made a difference in my life, and I knew I wanted to make a difference in somebody else's life."

Boser felt drawn to teaching and eventually to the principal role, where he could have "the opportunity to make a difference for each and every kid who walks through that door." It's that deep, abiding sense of moral purpose that keeps Boser, Andersen, and the other principals we profiled going, sometimes deep into the night, putting in the thankless hours required to do the job right, drawing upon a deep reservoir of conviction of doing something larger than themselves.

A Selfless, Iron Will to Improve Performance

The principals we interviewed all appeared to put their school's needs ahead of their own. In the business world, Jim Collins calls this "Level 5 leadership." While profiling dozens of companies that managed sustained improvement over many years, Collins found at the heart of them a "leader who is ambitious first and foremost for the cause, for the company, for the work, not for himself or herself; and has an absolutely terrifying iron will to make good on that ambition" (Crainer, 2006, n.p.).

In short, great leaders are not necessarily charismatic or bombastic. In fact, Collins found that when a company becomes too much a cult of personality, it tends to fail in the long term. A case in point is Chrysler under Lee Iacocca, who came in with great fanfare, putting himself on television ads and orchestrating Chrysler's meteoric rise in the 1980s, only to seek early retirement when the company's fortunes reversed in the early 1990s and eventually wind up in litigation with his former company. In contrast, Level 5 leaders tend to be the best leaders you've never heard of. They're humble yet incredibly driven. "They will do whatever it takes to make the company great," said Collins in an interview about his research (Crainer, 2006). "No matter how painful, no matter how emotionally stressing the decision has to be, they have the will to do it. It is that very unusual combination [that] separates out the Level 5 leaders."

What Collins found in great business leaders, we found in the school leaders who had taken Balanced Leadership to heart and carried the ideas into their practice.

Mike Andersen, for example, is a quiet leader who challenges and supports his staff at the same time. In our conversations with him, we learned that he cares primarily about one thing: providing the best, most relevant education possible to the 2,000 students of Barry Goldwater High School. It's an aspiration not for himself but for his community. And when asked what drew him to the principal position, his answer was insightful: "To lead change," he told us. Not to be principal. Not to run the high school. Not to keep a lid on problems, keep things running smoothly, or manage the building. His goal was to *lead change*.

Let's face it. Simply running a school can be a full-time job. A principal can spend all of his or her time overseeing the smoothest-running school in all 50 states—teacher satisfaction can be high, parents generally satisfied, discipline rates within reason, dropout rates better than the district or state levels—and yet continue to produce consistently flat, uninspiring student achievement results and continue to replicate so-so performance.

Great leaders, though, are never satisfied with the status quo. They're always looking for ways to improve, making waves if they have to. Andersen could have sat back, run his school smoothly and submitted paperwork to the district on time, and collected a paycheck. But he didn't. Instead he chose to make waves. Why? Because teachers were struggling and unhappy, says Andersen. Because students were "stumbling" out of high school. They weren't being "launched" into life the way Andersen imagined they should be.

And, finally, because the grading system was producing dishonest information about a student's capabilities. Despite the blowback, Andersen kept at it, with the iron will of a great leader.

Parker, Boyd, and Pasiewicz were the same. They were not satisfied with the current performance of their schools—or making excuses for the performances. They focused on supporting their teachers and helping them get a little better every day. These leaders viewed their school as human organizations and understood the critical importance of sharing leadership. They demonstrated the iron will to do whatever it takes to develop teachers and keep their schools moving on an upward trajectory.

A Deep Reservoir of Optimism

When talking to these leaders, we also noticed their can-do spirit and boundless optimism. They weren't being Pollyannas or shying away from inconvenient truths about their schools. Indeed, they could all point to opportunities to improve their data. And none hid the data—much of it was displayed on "data walls" in administrative offices or faculty lounges. Yet in almost the same breath that they highlighted concerns, they spoke optimistically about their collective ability to turn things around.

When John Parker told his staff about the increased rigor of the coming Common Core standards, he framed them as a challenge—one that would require everyone in the school to focus on developing students' close reading skills—but not an insurmountable one. Instead of lamenting the constant barrage of challenges, Parker looks beyond education to see that change is commonplace. "You look at a lot of businesses or industries, they are always having to reinvent themselves. Starbucks has to put a product out there for customers, yet they are always changing things up, always asking how they are going to meet the needs of their customers." Evergreen Middle School is no different.

In Sedalia, Colorado, George Boser seemed keenly aware of how his attitude affects his leadership—and the attitudes of those around him. "Your explanatory style stems directly from your view of your place in the world—whether you think you are valuable or deserving, or worthless and hopeless," said Boser. "It is the hallmark of whether you are an optimist or a pessimist." Boser's optimism translates into a belief that his school can be not just good but great. "Utopia," in fact, is the word he uses. "My job is to create the school you always talked about, where people collaborate and they push each other's thinking and they don't get offended when you say, 'Hey, have you tried this? Have you ever thought about that?' It's the kind of school where you can have hard conversations but it's only about getting better. You don't have to know everything, but you can rely on each other for support."

For Boser and the other strong leaders we met, the glass is always half full. And they're adding water.

Emotional Intelligence and Relationship Building

Two decades ago, Daniel Goleman (1995), then a science journalist with the *New York Times*, popularized a different kind of IQ, something called *emotional intelligence*. Goleman's four-part model of emotional intelligence included self-awareness, self-management, social awareness (or empathy), and relationship management. In subsequent work (1998/2004), he highlighted a strong link between emotional intelligence and leadership ability, noting that "without it, a person can have the best training in the world, an incisive, analytical mind, and an endless supply of smart ideas, but he still won't make a great leader." According to Goleman, emotional intelligence enables leaders to keep their emotions in check, to think before acting, to demonstrate a passion for their work, to pursue goals with energy and persistence, and—most relevant to communication—to persuade others by finding common ground and building rapport.

Following in the footsteps of Goleman and other business researchers, a growing number of studies have documented a strong link between school principals' emotional intelligence and their schools' performance (Labby, Lunenburg, & Slate, 2012). In 2005, Stone, Parker, and Wood examined a sample of 464 principals and vice principals and found that those whom teachers rated as having "above-average" leadership abilities also scored higher overall on an emotional intelligence survey. In particular, the most effective principals demonstrated high levels of self-awareness, self-actualization (the ability to engage in self-improvement), empathy, interpersonal relationship building, flexibility, problem solving, and impulse control.

More recently, Hanlin (2014) examined the extent to which the emotional intelligence of 66 high school principals predicted their ability to fulfill the 21 responsibilities of effective leaders in Balanced Leadership (Waters, Marzano, & McNulty, 2003). Her study found a strong positive correlation ($r = 0.74$) between emotional intelligence (in particular, the domains of self-monitoring and relationship building) and a number of key leadership responsibilities, including keeping goals at the forefront of everyone's attention, conveying strong convictions, regularly discussing best practices with staff, reading undercurrents in the school, advocating for the school with external stakeholders, being accessible to teachers, and keeping the lines of dialogue open.

We saw many of these same characteristics in the leaders we profiled. Eva Pasiewicz, for one, had a "road to Damascus" conversion moment when she realized that, as a leader, she had been neglecting the power of personal relationships. "I was bulldozing over [the staff]. I was saying 'This is how we're going to do things. Let's go for it.' Now it's 'Let's look at this. How can we move forward with this, and who is ready to move ahead and who needs a little more time?'"

Mike Andersen, on the other hand, always had a knack for getting along with people and creating relationships. But he began to see relationships as the basis of all organizations. The closest thing he had to a conversion moment was when, as a band director, he'd find himself in conversations with academic-subject-area teachers and notice a profound disconnect. "I would come to these monthly staff meetings with other teachers, and I would just hear these horror stories about everything, and I'm thinking, 'Where am I? I missed something here.' They were having problems with kids that I never experienced. I wondered if I could help them. That was the moment. I just saw so many teachers unhappy and struggling, and I couldn't figure out why, because I was in heaven." As a principal, Andersen became determined not only to have strong relationships with his colleagues, but also to help them to have strong, positive relationships with their students.

A Commitment to Self-Improvement

What may be most striking about the principals we profiled is that through long conversations with them, we realized that none self-describes as a natural-born leader. In fact, at some point in their careers, they took stock of their abilities and current practices as principals and realized they needed to grow as leaders.

At one point in her career, Eva Pasiewicz quit the job altogether and only hit her stride when she realized she need not be a top-down, directive leader; indeed, she could be more successful, over the long haul, by becoming an empowering leader and building a purposeful community. She still acknowledges that she needs to work on her situational awareness.

John Parker, a self-described Type A personality, realized that his strong management skills were necessary but insufficient. He was a great building manager but needed to work on becoming a great instructional leader. He immersed himself in developing deeper knowledge of curriculum, instruction, and assessment so that he could work alongside Janice Boyd, focusing their school on doing the right things. He admits he's still learning every day alongside—and sometimes from—his staff about effective instruction.

Mike Andersen will tell you he's hardly prone to motivational speaking or striking a "George Washington crossing the Delaware" type of pose. But after learning about the importance of creating demand for change, he learned how to leverage what he does best—ask sincere questions—into a leadership style that works for him and his school.

What all of this suggests is that no principal steps into the role on day one as the perfect leader. There's much to learn—and much that can be learned. And perhaps, more than anything else, that's the key message of this book—that leaders are not born but made.

Less Mystery, More Action

Mike Andersen said he was about halfway through a two-year immersion in Balanced Leadership training when he realized he could be an effective principal. Being able to see the component parts of leadership removed much of mystery of what it takes to be a great leader—showing that nurture, not just nature, has a lot to do with it. Andersen looked at many of the 21 responsibilities of strong school leaders and saw himself in them. Others offered opportunities for improvement. But because he now understood them, he could also see a path for getting better at them—and for reaching out to others on his team to help him with them, understanding that no person, or principal, is an island.

We hope that the research-based insights in these pages have helped you unpack the complexity of school leadership, removing perhaps some of the mystery of what it takes to be a great leader. We also hope the stories of real people (who would describe themselves as ordinary folks), applying these ideas in their schools, have shown that it's possible for you to do the same with your colleagues in your school. Finally, we hope that the practical tools in these pages can support a collaborative dialogue and an ongoing process of improvement in your school.

We believe that there is no leadership position that has the potential to do greater good than that of the school leader. To create a better world, we need school leaders with the skills and acumen to keep their schools focused, to manage the complex changes inherent in focusing on student learning, and to build the resilient and purposeful communities needed to withstand and even thrive in times of innovation and change. It is our sincerest hope that the stories, tools, and knowledge found in this book might provide guidance for the current and next generation of school leaders, ready to take on the challenges that lie ahead.

Moreover, we believe that it's possible for ordinary people to do extraordinary things when they understand the science and art of their profession and work together to accomplish great things. On that note, if you're the only one in your school reading this book, we encourage you to hand it to one of your colleagues to read as well. School leadership is too big and too important for anyone to go it alone. Sure, with heroic efforts, a single noble leader can make a difference. You might even get some quick wins and pats on the back from your administrators and colleagues. Ultimately, your efforts will not be sustainable—and they will be exhausting.

Remember, continuous school improvement is not a sprint but a marathon—and a race best run not alone but with others. In the end, the guidance for school leaders that we offer in this book might best be summed up by the old African proverb: If you want to go fast, go alone; if you want to go far, go together.

Enjoy your journey together.

Appendix:
The 21 Balanced Leadership Responsibilities and 66 Associated Practices

RESPONSIBILITY	AVERAGE r	THE EXTENT TO WHICH THE PRINCIPAL . . .	ASSOCIATED PRACTICES
Affirmation	.19	Recognizes and celebrates school accomplishments and acknowledges failures	• Systematically and fairly recognizes the accomplishments of teachers and staff • Systematically and fairly recognizes and celebrates the accomplishments of students • Systematically and fairly recognizes the failures of and celebrates the accomplishments of the school as a whole
Change Agent	.25	Is willing to challenge and actively challenges the status quo	• Consciously challenges the status quo • Is willing to lead change initiatives with uncertain outcomes • Systematically considers new and better ways of doing things • Consistently attempts to operate at the edge versus the center of the school's competence
Communication	.23	Establishes strong lines of communication with and among teachers and students	• Is easily accessible to teachers and staff • Develops effective means for teachers and staff to communicate with one another • Maintains open and effective lines of communication with teachers and staff
Contingent Rewards	.24	Recognizes and rewards individual accomplishments	• Uses performance versus seniority as the primary criterion for rewards and recognition • Uses hard work and results as the basis for rewards and recognition • Recognizes individuals who excel

RESPONSIBILITY	AVERAGE r	THE EXTENT TO WHICH THE PRINCIPAL . . .	ASSOCIATED PRACTICES
Culture	.25	Fosters shared beliefs and a sense of community and cooperation	• Promotes a sense of well-being among teachers and staff • Promotes cohesion among teachers and staff • Develops an understanding of purpose among teachers and staff • Develops a shared vision of what the school could be like • Promotes cooperation among teachers and staff
Discipline	.27	Protects teachers from issues and influences that would detract from their teaching time or focus	• Protects instructional time from interruptions • Protects/shelters teachers and staff from internal and external distractions
Flexibility	.28	Adapts his or her leadership behavior to the needs of the current situation and is comfortable with dissent	• Is comfortable with making major changes in how things are done • Encourages people to express diverse opinions contrary to those held by individuals in positions of authority • Adapts leadership style to the needs of specific situations • Is directive or nondirective as the situation warrants
Focus	.24	Establishes clear goals and keeps those goals in the forefront of the school's attention	• Establishes high, concrete goals and expectations that all students meet those goals. • Establishes high, concrete goals for curriculum, instruction, and assessment practices within the school • Establishes high, concrete goals for the general functioning of the school • Continually keeps attention on established goals
Ideals and Beliefs	.22	Communicates and operates from strong ideals and beliefs about schooling	• Possesses well-defined beliefs about schools, teaching, and learning • Shares beliefs about schools, teaching, and learning with the teachers and staff • Demonstrates behaviors that are consistent with beliefs
Input	.25	Involves teachers in the design and implementation of important decisions and policies	• Provides opportunities for teacher and staff input on all important decisions • Provides opportunities for teachers and staff to be involved in developing school policies • Uses leadership teams in decision making

RESPONSIBILITY	AVERAGE r	THE EXTENT TO WHICH THE PRINCIPAL . . .	ASSOCIATED PRACTICES
Intellectual Stimulation	.24	Ensures faculty and staff are aware of the most current theories and practices and makes the discussion of these a regular aspect of the school culture	• Keeps informed about current research and theory on effective schooling • Continually exposes teachers and staff to cutting-edge research and theory on effective schooling • Fosters systematic discussion regarding current research and theory on effective schooling
Involvement in Curriculum, Instruction, and Assessment	.20	Is directly involved in the design and implementation of curriculum, instruction, and assessment practices	• Is directly involved in helping teachers design curricular activities and address assessment and instructional issues
Knowledge of Curriculum, Instruction, and Assessment	.25	Is knowledgeable about current curriculum, instruction, and assessment practices	• Possesses extensive knowledge about effective curricular, instructional, and assessment practices • Provides conceptual guidance regarding effective classroom practices
Monitor and Evaluate	.27	Monitors the effectiveness of school practices and their impact on student learning	• Continually monitors the effectiveness of the school's curricular practices • Continually monitors the effectiveness of the school's instructional practices • Continually monitors the effectiveness of the school's assessment practices • Remains aware of the impact of the school's practices on student achievement
Optimize	.20	Inspires and leads new and challenging innovations	• Inspires teachers and staff to accomplish things that might be beyond their grasp • Is the driving force behind major initiatives • Portrays a positive attitude about the ability of teachers and staff to accomplish substantial things
Order	.25	Establishes a set of standard operating procedures and routines	• Provides and reinforces clear structures, rules, and procedures for teachers and staff • Provides and reinforces clear structures, rules, and procedures for students • Establishes routines for the effective running of the school that teachers and staff understand and follow
Outreach	.27	Is an advocate and spokesperson for the school to all stakeholders	• Ensures the school complies with all district and state mandates • Is an advocate of the school with the community at large • Is an advocate of the school with parents • Is an advocate of the school with central office

RESPONSIBILITY	AVERAGE r	THE EXTENT TO WHICH THE PRINCIPAL . . .	ASSOCIATED PRACTICES
Relationships	.18	Demonstrates awareness of the personal aspects of teachers and staff	• Is informed about significant personal issues within the lives of teachers and staff • Maintains personal relationships with teachers and staff • Is aware of the personal needs of teachers and staff • Acknowledges significant events in the lives of teachers and staff
Resources	.25	Provides teachers with materials and professional development necessary for the successful execution of their jobs	• Ensures that teachers and staff have the necessary materials and equipment • Ensures that teachers and staff have the necessary professional development opportunities that directly enhance their teaching
Situational Awareness	.33	Is aware of the details and the undercurrents in the running of the school and uses this information to address current and potential problems	• Is aware of informal groups and relationships among teachers and staff • Is aware of the issues in the school that have not surfaced but could create discord • Accurately predicts what could go wrong from day to day
Visibility	.20	Has quality contacts and interactions with teachers and students	• Makes systematic and frequent visits to the classroom • Is highly visible to students, teachers, and parents • Has frequent contact with students

*Note: The correlation coefficient, or r, ranges from −1.0 to +1.0. A number closer to +1 indicates that, as one variable gets larger, the other gets larger. Therefore, the larger the r number, the stronger the correlation, or relationship, between the leadership responsibility and overall student achievement.

Source: Adapted from School Leadership That Works: From Research to Results (pp. 42–43), by R. J. Marzano, T. Waters, & B. A. McNulty, 2005, Alexandria, VA: Association for Supervision and Curriculum Development. Copyright © 2005 by Mid-continent Research for Education and Learning (McREL).

References

Bandura, A. (1997). *Self-efficacy: The exercise of control*. New York: W. H. Freeman.

Barber, M., & Mourshed, M. (2007). *How the world's best-performing school systems come out on top*. London: McKinsey.

Béteille, T., Kalogrides, D., & Loeb, S. (2011). Stepping stones: Principal career paths and school outcomes [Working paper 17243]. Cambridge, MA: National Bureau of Economic Research. Retrieved from http://www.nber.org/papers/w17243

Bridges, W. (1991). *Managing transitions: Making the most of change*. Reading, MA: Addison-Wesley.

Bronson, P., & Merryman, A. (2013). *Top dog: The science of winning and losing*. New York: Twelve.

Bryk, A. S., Sebring, P. B., Allensworth, E., Luppescu, S., & Easton, J. Q. (2010). *Organizing schools for improvement: Lessons from Chicago*. Chicago: University of Chicago Press.

Bryk, A. S., Sebring, P. B., Kerbow, D., Rollow, S., & Easton, J. Q. (1998). *Charting Chicago school reform: Democratic localism as a lever for change*. Boulder, CO: Westview Press.

Buckingham, M. & Clifton, D. O. (2001). *Now, discover your strengths*. New York: Free Press.

Burkhauser, S., Gates, S., Hamilton, L. S., & Ikemoto, G. S. (2012). *First-year principals in urban school districts: How actions and working conditions relate to outcomes*. Santa Monica, CA: RAND Corp.

Central Washington University. (2014). *CWU teacher time study: How Washington public school teachers spend their work days*. Ellensburg, WA: Author. http://www.cwu.edu/sites/default/files/images/teachertimestudy.pdf

Chenoweth, K. (2007). *"It's being done": Academic success in unexpected schools*. Cambridge, MA: Harvard Education Publishing Group.

Chenoweth, K. (2009). *How it's being done: Urgent lessons from unexpected schools*. Cambridge, MA: Harvard Education Press.

Crainer, S. (2006, January 3). Interview: Jim Collins and Level 5 Leadership. Retrieved from http://www.management-issues.com/2006/5/24/mentors/jim-collins-and-level-5-leadership.asp

Dean, C., Hubbell, E., Pitler, H., & Stone, B. (2012). *Classroom instruction that works* (2nd ed.). Alexandria, VA: ASCD.

Deutschman, A. (2006). *Change or die: The three keys to change at work and in life*. New York: HarperBusiness.

Drummond, K., Chinen, M., Duncan, T. G., Miller, H. R., Fryer, L., Zmach, C., & Culp, K. (2011). *Impact of the Thinking Reader software program on grade 6 reading vocabulary, comprehension, strategies, and motivation* (NCEE 2010-4035). Washington, DC: National Center for Education Evaluation and Regional Assistance.

Elmore, R. (2002). *Bridging the gap between standards and improvement: The imperative for professional development in education.* Washington, DC: Albert Shanker Institute.

Finn, C. E. (2012, April 4). Why school principals need more authority. *The Atlantic.* Available at http://www.theatlantic.com/national/archive/2012/04/why-school-principals-need-more-authority/255183/

Fullan, M. (2011). Choosing the wrong drivers for whole system reform. Summary of Seminar Series Paper No. 204. Melbourne, Australia: Centre for Strategic Education.

Fuller, E. (2012, July 16). Examining principal turnover [blog post]. Retrieved from http://www.shankerinstitute.org/blog/examining-principal-turnover.

Gamson, W., & Lasch, K. (1982). The political culture of social welfare policy. In S. E. Spiro & E. Yuchtman-Yaar (Eds.), *Social policy evaluation: Social political perspective* (pp. 397–415). New York: Academic Press.

Goddard, R. D. (2001). Collective efficacy: A neglected construct in the study of schools and achievement. *Journal of Educational Psychology, 93*(3), 467–476.

Goddard, R. (2002). A theoretical and empirical analysis of the measurement of collective efficacy: The development of a short form. *Educational and Psychological Measurement, 62*(1), 97–110.

Goddard, R. D., Hoy, W. K., & Hoy, A. W. (2000). Collective teacher efficacy: Its meaning, measure, and impact on student achievement. *American Educational Research Journal, 37*(2), 479–507.

Goddard, R. D., Hoy, W. K., & Hoy, A. W. (2004). Collective efficacy beliefs: Theoretical developments, empirical evidence, and future directions. *Educational Researcher, 33*(3), 3–13.

Goleman, D. (1995). *Emotional intelligence.* New York: Bantam.

Goleman, D. (1998/2004). What makes a leader? *Harvard Business Review* (January 2004). Retrieved from https://hbr.org/2004/01/what-makes-a-leader

Goodwin, B. (2011a, October). Research says: Implementation counts. *Educational Leadership, 69*(2) 82–83.

Goodwin, B. (2011b). *Simply better: Doing what matters most to change the odds for student success.* Alexandria, VA: ASCD.

Gross, J. A. (2014). 5 whys folklore: The truth behind a monumental mystery. Retrieved from http://thekaizone.com/2014/08/5-whys-folklore-the-truth-behind-a-monumental-mystery/

Hanlin, D. C. (2014). *The relationship between emotional intelligence and research-based leadership practices of high school principals* [Unpublished dissertation]. College Park, MD: University of Maryland.

Heath, C., & Heath, D. (2010). *Switch: How to change things when change is hard.* New York: Crown Business.

Heifetz, R. A., & Laurie, D. L. (1997). The work of leadership. *Harvard Business Review, 75*(1), 124–134.

Heifetz, R. A., & Linsky, M. (2002). *Leadership on the line: Staying alive through the dangers of leading.* Boston: Harvard Business School Press.

Hopkins, D., & Craig, W. (2011). Powerful learning: Taking education reform to scale in the Northern Metropolitan Region. In D. Hopkins, W. Craig, & J. Munro (Eds.), *Powerful learning: A strategy for systemic educational improvement* (pp. 28–37). Melbourne, Australia: ACER Press.

Hoy, W. K., Smith, P. A., & Sweetland, S. R. (2002). A test of a model of school achievement in rural schools: The significance of collective efficacy. In W. K. Hoy & C. Miskel (Eds.), *Theory and research in educational administration: Vol. 1* (pp. 185–202). Greenwich, CT: Information Age Publishing.

Hoy, W. K., Tarter, C. J., & Hoy, A. W. (2006). Academic optimism of schools: A force for student achievement. *American Educational Research Journal, 43*(3), 425–446.

Iyengar, S., & Lepper, M. (2000).When choice is demotivating: Can one desire too much of a good thing? *Journal of Personality and Social Psychology, 79*(6), 995–1006.

Jacob, R., Goddard, R., Kim, M., Miller, R., & Goddard, Y. (2014, September). Exploring the causal impact of the McREL Balanced Leadership program on leadership, principal efficacy, instructional climate, educator turnover, and student achievement. *Educational Evaluation and Policy Analysis*, 1–19.

Johnson, L. A. (2005). Why principals quit. *Principal, 84*(3), 21–23.

Joyce, B., & Showers, B. (2002). Student achievement through professional development. In B. Joyce & B. Showers (Eds.), *Designing training and peer coaching: Our need for learning.* Alexandria, VA: Association for Supervision and Curriculum Development.

Kaplan, R. S., & Norton, D. P. (2004). Measuring the strategic readiness of intangible assets. *Harvard Business Review OnPoint Collection*, 13–27.

Konstantopoulos, S. (2005). Trends of school effects on student achievement: Evidence from NLS:72, HSB:82, and NELS:92 (p. 1). Bonn, Germany: Institute for the Study of Labor.

Kushman, J., Hanita, M., & Raphael, J. (2011). *An experimental study of the Project CRISS reading program on grade 9 reading achievement in rural high schools* (NCEE 2010-4007). Washington, DC: National Center for Education Evaluation and Regional Assistance.

Labby, S., Lundberg, F. C., & Slate, J. R. (2012). Emotional intelligence and academic success: A conceptual analysis for educational leaders. *International Journal of Educational Leadership Preparation, 7*(1).

Lorinkova, N. M., Pearsall, M. J., & Sims, H. P. (2013). Examining the differential longitudinal performance of directive versus empowering leadership in teams. *Academy of Management Journal, 56*(2), 573–596.

Low, J., & Kalafut, P. C. (2002). *Invisible advantage: How intangibles are driving business performance.* New York: Basic Books.

Martella, R., Nelson, J., & Marchand-Martella, N. (2003). *Managing disruptive behaviors in schools.* Boston: Pearson.

Marzano, R. J. (2000). *A new era of school reform: Going where the research takes us.* Aurora, CO: McREL.

Marzano, R. J., Waters, T. (2009). *District leadership that works: Striking the right balance.* Bloomington, IN: Solution Tree.

Marzano, R. J., Waters, J. T., & McNulty, B. A. (2005). *School leadership that works: From research to results.* Alexandria, VA: ASCD.

McFarland, K. (2009). *Bounce: The art of turning tough times into triumph.* New York: Crown Business.

McREL. (2005). *McREL Insights: Schools that "beat the odds."* Aurora, CO: Author.

National Center for Education Statistics. (1997). *Time spent teaching core academic subjects in elementary schools: Comparisons across community, school, teacher, and student characteristics* (NCES 97-293). Washington, DC: U.S. Department of Education, Office of Educational Research and Improvement.

National Center on Time and Learning. (2011). *Time well spent: Eight powerful practices of successful, expanded-time schools.* Washington, DC: Author.

Paek, P. L. (2008, January). Asset-based instruction: Boston Public Schools [Case study from *Practices worthy of attention: Local innovations in strengthening secondary mathematics*]. Austin, TX: Charles A. Dana Center at the University of Texas at Austin.

Pan, D., Rudo, Z. H., Schneider, C. L., & Smith-Hansen, L. (2003, April). *Examination of resource allocation in education: Connecting spending to student performance.* Austin, TX: Southwest Educational Development Laboratory.

Payne, C. M. (2008). *So much reform, so little change: The persistence of failure in urban schools.* Cambridge, MA: Harvard Education Press.

Pink, D. H. (2009). *Drive: The surprising truth about what motivates us.* New York: Riverhead Books.

Public Impact. (2008). *School turnaround leaders: Competencies for success.* Public Impact for the Chicago Public Education Fund. Chapel Hill, NC: Author.

Resar, R., Griffin F. A., Haraden, C., & Nolan, T. W. (2012). *Using care bundles to improve health care quality.* [IHI Innovation Series white paper]. Cambridge, MA: Institute for Healthcare Improvement.

Robinson, V. M. J., Lloyd, C. A., & Rowe, K. J. (2008). The impact of leadership on student outcomes: An analysis of the differential effects of leadership types. *Educational Administration Quarterly, 44*(5), 635–674.

Rogers, E. M. (2003). *Diffusion of innovations* (5th ed.). New York: Free Press.

Rowe, M. B. (1986). Wait time: Slowing down may be a way of speeding up! *Journal of Teacher Education, 37*(1), 43–50.

Schmoker, M. (2011). *Focus: Elevating the essentials to radically improve student learning.* Alexandria, VA: ASCD.

Seashore-Louis, K., Leithwood, K., Wahlstrom, K. L., & Anderson, S. E. (2010). *Learning from leadership: Investigating the links to improved student learning* [Final Report of Research to the Wallace Foundation]. Minneapolis, MN: University of Minnesota.

Seligman, M. E. P. (1990). *Learned optimism: How to change your mind and your life.* New York: Free Press.

Sinek, S. (2011). *Start with why.* New York: Portfolio.

Somech, A. (2006). The effects of leadership style and team process on performance and innovation in functionally heterogeneous teams. *Journal of Management, 32*(1), 132–157.

Stone, H., Parker, J. D., & Wood, L. M. (2005). *Report on the Ontario Principals' Council leadership study.* Retrieved from www.eiconsortium.org/pdf/opc_leadership_study_final_report.pdf

Stringfield, S., Reynolds, D., & Schaffer, G. (2010). *Toward highly reliable, high quality public schooling.* Paper presented at the McREL Best in the World Consortium meeting, Denver, CO.

Ulrich, D., & Smallwood, N. (2004, June). Capitalizing on capabilities. *Harvard Business Review, (82)*6, 119–127, 138.

U.S. Department of Education, National Center for Education Evaluation and Regional Assistance, Institute of Education Sciences. (2009). *Assisting students struggling with reading: Response to Intervention (RtI) and multi-tier intervention in the primary grades.* Washington, DC: Author.

Walberg, H. J. (1984). Improving the productivity of America's schools. *Educational Leadership, 41*(8), 19–27.

Waters, T., & Cameron, G. (2007). *The Balanced Leadership framework: Connecting vision with action.* Aurora, CO: McREL.

Waters, J. T., Marzano, R. J., & McNulty, B. (2003). *Balanced leadership: What 30 years of research tells us about the effect of leadership on student achievement.* Aurora, CO: McREL.

Weick, K. (1982). Administering education in loosely coupled schools. *Phi Delta Kappan, 63*(10), 673–676.

Yosso, T. J. (2005). Whose culture has capital? A critical race theory discussion of community cultural wealth. *Race, Ethnicity and Education, 8*(1), 69–91.

About the Authors

 **Bryan Goodwin** is the president and CEO of McREL International, a Denver-based nonprofit education research and development organization. Goodwin, a former teacher and journalist, has been at McREL for 15 years, serving previously as Chief Operating Officer and Director of Communications and Marketing. He has authored or coauthored several books, including *Simply Better: Doing What Matters Most to Change the Odds for Student Success*, *The 12 Touchstones of Good Teaching: A Checklist for Staying Focused Every Day*, and *The Future of Schooling: Educating America in 2020*. Goodwin writes a monthly research column for *Educational Leadership* and presents research findings and insights to audiences across the United States and in Canada and Australia. He can be reached at bgoodwin@mcrel.org.

 **Greg Cameron** is an educational leader and consultant and former executive director at McREL International, where he provided oversight and support for McREL's school-level leadership work. From 2002 to 2015, he served on the organization's leadership design and developmental team, designing and facilitating high-quality professional development for school leaders across the United States and around the world. Cameron is co-author of *The Balanced Leadership Framework* and *Teaching Reading in Social Studies*. Previously, he was an elementary school principal, an assistant principal, and a middle and high school classroom teacher. Cameron can be reached at gregcmrn@gmail.com.

 **Heather Hein** is a communications consultant at McREL International. For the past decade, she has written and edited a variety of publications and materials that engage educators in McREL's work. Hein has taught English as a second language to adults and has worked as a journalist; she now serves as managing editor of McREL's magazine, *Changing Schools*, and provides editorial support and guidance for the organization. She can be reached at hhein@mcrel.org.

About McREL

McREL International is an internally recognized, nonprofit education research and development organization, headquartered in Denver, Colorado; with offices in Honolulu, Hawai'i; Nashville, Tennesee; Charleston, West Virginia; and Melbourne, Australia. Since 1966, McREL has helped translate research and professional wisdom about what works in education into practical guidance for educators. Our 120-plus staff members and affiliates include respected researchers, experienced consultants, and published writers who provide educators with research-based guidance, consultation, and professional development for improving student outcomes. Contact us if you have questions or comments or would like to arrange a presentation, workshop, or other assistance from McREL in applying the ideas from this book in your district, school, or classroom.

Related ASCD Resources: School Leadership

At the time of publication, the following ASCD resources were available (ASCD stock numbers appear in parentheses). For up-to-date information about ASCD resources, go to www.ascd. org. You can search the complete archives of *Educational Leadership* at http://www.ascd.org/el.

Books

The Art of School Leadership by Thomas R. Hoerr (#105037)

Improving Student Learning One Principal at a Time by Jane E. Pollock and Sharon M. Ford (#109006)

Insights into Action: Successful School Leaders Share What Works by William Sterrett (#109019)

Leading Change in Your School: How to Conquer Myths, Build Commitment, and Get Results by Douglas B. Reeves (#109019)

Learning from Lincoln: Leadership Practices for School Success by Harvey Alvy and Pam Robbins (#110036)

The Learning Leader: How to Focus School Improvement for Better Results by Douglas B. Reeves (#105151)

The New Principal's Fieldbook: Strategies for Success by Pam Robbins and Harvey Alvy (#103019)

Resilient School Leaders: Strategies for Turning Adversity Into Achievement by Jerry L. Patterson and Paul Kelleher (#104003)

Schooling by Design: Mission, Action, and Achievement by Grant Wiggins and Jay McTighe (#107018)

School Leadership That Works: From Research To Results by Robert J. Marzano, Timothy Waters, and Brian A. McNulty (#105125)

Simply Better: Doing What Matters Most to Change the Odds for Student Success by Bryan Goodwin (#111038)

What Works in Schools: Translating Research into Action by Robert J. Marzano (#102271)

Networks

Visit the ASCD Web site (www.ascd.org) and click on About ASCD. Click on Networks, then Network Directory, for information about professional educators who have formed groups around topics, including "Teacher and Principal Evaluation" and "Performance Assessment in Leadership."

The Whole Child Initiative helps schools and communities create learning environments that allow students to be healthy, safe, engaged, supported, and challenged. To learn more about other books and resources that relate to the whole child, visit www.wholechildeducation.org.

For more information: send e-mail to member@ascd.org; call 1-800-933-2723 or 703-578-9600, press 2; send a fax to 703-575-5400; or write to Information Services, ASCD, 1703 N. Beauregard St., Alexandria, VA 22311-1714 USA.